CIAO!

CIAO BISCOTTI
★★

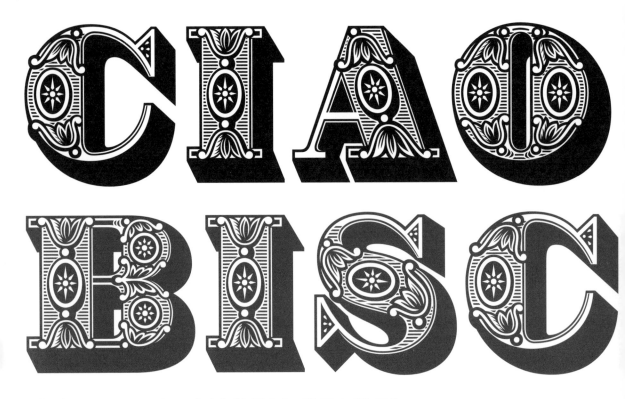

CIAO BISC

SWEET AND SAVORY RECIPES
CELEBRATING ITALY'S FAVORITE COOKIE

DOLCI

DOMENICA MARCHETTI

PHOTOGRAPHS BY **ANTONIS ACHILLEOS**

CHRONICLE BOOKS

SAN FRANCISCO

Library of Congress Cataloging-in-Publication Data:
Marchetti, Domenica.
  Ciao Biscotti : sweet and savory recipes celebrating Italy's favorite
cookie /by Domenica Marchetti ; photographs by Antonis Achilleos.
      pages cm
  Includes index.
ISBN 978-1-4521-2495-7
1. Biscotti. 2. Cooking, Italian. I. Title.

 TX772.M276 2015
 641.86'54—dc23

                    2014006991

Manufactured in China

MIX
Paper from
responsible sources
FSC® C008047

Designed by **VANESSA DINA**
Prop styling by **SPORK AND REPRO DEPOT**
Food styling by **ROBYN LENZI**
Typesetting by **DC TYPOGRAPHY**

Toblerone is a registered trademark of Kraft Foods Inc.
Nutella is a registered trademark of Ferrero.

10 9 8 7 6 5 4 3 2 1

Chronicle Books LLC
680 Second Street
San Francisco, California 94107

WWW.CHRONICLEBOOKS.COM

BUON APPETITO!

CONTENTS
★★★

One of life's pleasures is sitting down to a cup of coffee and a plate of biscotti.

These twice-baked Italian cookies are known and loved the world over, and with good reason. They are *the* perfect dunking cookie, satisfyingly crunchy and crumbly, not too sweet, and chock-full of nuts.

Surprisingly, I did not grow up eating biscotti in my Italian family. My mother preferred the thin, crisp embossed pizzelle that are a specialty of her native Abruzzo, and I myself was always in search of a better chocolate chip cookie. It wasn't until the 1980s or 1990s, when biscotti conquered the U.S. palate, that I started baking and truly appreciating this classic sweet.

Bite into a biscotto and you are biting into a slice of Italian—or, more accurately, Roman—history. It was during Roman times that bakers developed the technique of baking loaves of unleavened dough two times, once to cook them and once to dry them out—hence the term, from the words *bis* (twice) and *cotti* (cooked). With all the moisture baked out of them, biscotti lasted indefinitely and, in fact, were said to have nourished the traveling Roman troops. It's a good bet that those early versions of biscotti were closer to hardtack than to the fancy nut-filled, chocolate-drizzled cookies that we see today, artfully arranged in curvy glass jars at *pasticcerie* throughout Italy and at bakeries and coffee shops around the world.

For that transformation we can thank Tuscan pastry chef Antonio Mattei, who in 1858 set up shop in the town of Prato and began selling cookies based on a centuries-old recipe. His original ingredients were flour, sugar, eggs, and pine nuts or almonds from nearby groves. There was no additional leavening; the eggs were whisked at length with sugar to incorporate air into the dough. The soft, nut-studded dough was shaped into loaves, baked, sliced, and baked again into crunchy oblongs. Mattei's biscotti won prizes at food expos in Florence in 1861 and Paris in 1867. To this day, Biscottificio Antonio Mattei continues to turn out thousands upon thousands of its founder's sweet, crunchy creations, packaged in signature waxed blue paper bags.

In Tuscany, the preferred way to serve these traditional biscotti is not with coffee but rather with a glass of Vin Santo, the region's famed sweet dessert wine made from dried grapes.

Personally, I like biscotti with either beverage, and I wouldn't say no to a glass of cold milk as a dunking medium, either.

Over the generations, tradition has given way to interpretation and inspiration, so that now we have riffs on biscotti from all over Italy and around the globe. There are spiced biscotti; chocolate biscotti and chocolate chip biscotti; biscotti with hazelnuts, walnuts, and macadamia nuts; and biscotti studded with dried currants or apricots. Some are made tender with butter or olive oil, and some are gilded with drizzles of white or bittersweet chocolate. It's hard to fault the innovators. While I respect, even revere, traditional recipes, I can't imagine not playing around with a recipe as malleable and as open to interpretation as the one for biscotti.

And that is what I've been doing in my kitchen for the past couple of decades since I baked my first batch. The result is this book, a collection of my favorite biscotti recipes. It includes recipes that I have gathered over the years from family and friends, from my travels to Italy, and from my own scribbled notebooks. In these pages you'll find everything from classic, bite-size almond biscotti to extra-large cappuccino dunkers; and from sweet iced triple lemon biscotti to savory Gorgonzola and walnut biscotti.

The book is organized simply, beginning with "Biscotti Basics," which includes a list of necessary equipment and ingredients, plus a helpful section of techniques for baking perfect biscotti. The chapters that follow are the heart of the book: "Classic Flavors," "Chocolate and Spice," "Biscotti with Fruit," "Fantasy Flavors," and "The Savory Side." A final bonus chapter, "Beyond Biscotti," features select recipes for a handful of my *other* favorite Italian cookies, including hazelnut meringues, tender jam-filled crescents, and chewy almond ricciarelli. With every recipe you'll find a suggested beverage pairing. For this I must tip my hat to Italian wine and drink aficionado Scott Vance (who also happens to be my husband).

Perhaps the most appealing feature of biscotti is that they so beautifully, and sweetly, express that unique Italian blend of sophistication and rustic charm. You can dunk them in your morning cappuccino, pack them in a picnic basket, or serve them on fancy dessert plates at the end of an elegant dinner.

So pour yourself a glass of Vin Santo—or a cup of coffee—and together let's celebrate yet another one of Italy's delicious contributions to the culinary world—biscotti!

BISCOTTI BASICS

A WORD ABOUT THE WORD *BISCOTTI*

A certain amount of confusion surrounds the word *biscotti*, so I'd like to clear that up. The word derives from the Latin *biscotus*, meaning "twice baked." In Italy, the word *biscotti* has come to be a catchall term for cookies. The specific twice-baked cookies originating in Antonio Mattei's bakery in Prato are more commonly known as *biscotti di Prato* or *cantucci di Prato*. You may even have come across the term *cantuccini*, which is simply a diminutive form of *cantucci*, and refers to the tapered end pieces of a sliced loaf of biscotti, which are smaller than those sliced from the middle. In this book, I have reserved the term *cantucci* for the most traditional recipes and went with *biscotti* for all the others. Finally, the word *biscotti* is already plural, so there is no need to add an *s* (biscottis). The singular form of the word is *biscotto*.

Making biscotti is easy once you get the hang of it. The first rule, of course, is to relax and have fun—you're making biscotti! The next rule is to read this chapter, which contains an explanation of the equipment and ingredients you'll need, plus essential information on techniques from roasting nuts to handling and shaping sticky biscotti dough and creating the perfect drizzle on your biscotti.

Be sure also to read through the whole recipe before you start baking. Do any prep work, such as toasting or chopping nuts and measuring out flour and sugar, before you start so that you won't have to scramble when it comes time to mix everything together.

EQUIPMENT

You don't need a lot of fancy baking equipment to make great biscotti. You probably have most of what you need already. Following is an alphabetical list of tools and equipment that I have found useful in baking the biscotti in this book.

BAKING SHEETS

I use large, heavy-gauge aluminum, rimmed baking sheets (11 by 17 in/ 28 by 43 cm) to bake biscotti and the other cookies in this book.

COOKIE TINS

Biscotti are best stored in a metal tin with a tight-fitting lid, where they will stay fresh and crispy for about a week at room temperature. Those made without butter or oil will last even longer. I have stored biscotti in the freezer, but find they tend to absorb moisture and lose their appealing crunch.

COOLING RACKS
Two metal grid racks (10 by 18 in/ 25 by 46 cm) are enough to hold several dozen biscotti.

CUTTING BOARD
A sturdy wooden or plastic cutting board is a good surface for slicing biscotti.

DOUBLE BOILER
I bought an old, enamel-coated double boiler at a flea market years ago and find it's perfect for melting chocolate. You can also make your own: pour water about 2 in/5 cm deep into a medium saucepan, and then place a metal bowl over the water so that the bottom of the bowl does not touch the water. Heat the water to a low simmer and melt the chocolate gently in the bowl.

FOOD PROCESSOR
A couple of recipes in this book call for finely chopping or grinding nuts. A food processor makes quick work of this task.

KNIVES
I use a Santoku knife to slice biscotti. A serrated bread knife also works well. I also use the Santoku knife or a chef's knife to chop herbs and nuts and to cut dried fruit into small pieces. See page 18 for specific information on how to slice biscotti without causing them to break or crumble.

METRIC SCALE
A metric scale is useful for accurately measuring flour, sugar, nuts, and other ingredients. I have one that conveniently toggles between metric and imperial measurements, making conversion easy.

OFFSET METAL SPATULA
The thin, flat, angled blade of this standard baking tool is perfect for sliding under the baked biscotti loaf and lifting it off the baking sheet.

PASTRY BRUSH
I use a bristled pastry brush for coating baking pans with oil and for brushing the tops of biscotti loaves with egg wash.

SILICONE SPATULAS
A sturdy wooden-handled silicone spatula is helpful for scraping thick biscotti batter from the sides of the mixing bowl.

STAND MIXER
All the biscotti recipes in this book call for an electric stand mixer to mix the ingredients for biscotti dough. The dough is generally too sticky and dense for a handheld mixer to do the job properly.

WAX PAPER
Lining your baking sheets with wax paper before drizzling icing over your biscotti catches drips and helps to minimize mess.

WHISK

I use a hand whisk to combine dry ingredients and to mix ingredients for glazes. A whisk can also be dipped in glaze to be drizzled over biscotti.

INGREDIENTS

BUTTER

I prefer unsalted butter for baking because it allows me to control the amount of salt I want to add to the recipe. Most recipes in this book call for the butter to be brought to cool room temperature. It should be pliable but still a little cool to the touch.

CHOCOLATE

Bittersweet, semisweet, milk, and white chocolates are all used in recipes in this book. Bittersweet and semisweet both contain sugar, but bittersweet contains a higher percentage of cocoa liquor and less sugar. For the recipes in this book, these two chocolates can be used interchangeably.

CITRUS

A number of the recipes call for fresh lemon, lime, or orange zest. To avoid any possible residues from pesticides, I recommend using organic citrus.

COCONUT

A few recipes call for coconut. Use unsweetened if you can find it, as it tastes much more like coconut than the sweetened stuff. See page 16 for instructions on how to toast coconut.

EGGS

All of the recipes call for large eggs. If you can, buy eggs from a local farm, preferably where chickens are raised on organic feed. I find these have the freshest flavor.

EXTRACTS

Many recipes in this book call for flavor in the form of an extract—almond, lemon, orange, and vanilla among them. Use pure extracts rather than artificially flavored ones, which are manufactured from chemicals designed to mimic the taste and aroma of an ingredient but that rarely taste as good as the real thing. For anise flavor, I use an anise liqueur such as sambuca or Pernod, but pure anise extract may be substituted.

FLOUR

Most of the recipes in this book call for unbleached all-purpose flour. Several also call for the addition of other flours for extra texture and flavor, including almond, barley, spelt, and whole-wheat. Almond flour is also marketed as almond meal and is, essentially, very finely ground almonds. For the

Ricciarelli on page 138, be sure to use almond flour made from blanched (peeled) almonds. One recipe, Oil and Wine Tarallucci (page 134), calls for Italian "oo" flour. This is finely milled, soft wheat flour and is typically used to make fresh pasta. It contributes to the delicate, flaky character of the jam-filled tarallucci. Substitute unbleached all-purpose flour if you are unable to find "oo" flour.

MARSALA

Named for its city of origin in Sicily, Marsala is a fortified blended wine that can be sweet, medium-dry, or dry. The recipes in this book call for dry Marsala.

NUTS

Almonds and hazelnuts are what you will find in most biscotti. But why stop there? I've included recipes that contain pistachios, walnuts, pecans, and even peanuts. Almonds are sometimes added raw, but in general I prefer toasting nuts (see page 16) prior to adding them to biscotti dough.

OIL

A mild vegetable oil should be used to coat the baking pans. I like sunflower oil; it is light in flavor and is used often in Italian cooking and frying. For recipes that call for olive oil, I use good-quality extra-virgin olive oil. Look for labels that include either a harvest date or an expiration date and that specify where the olives are from and where the oil was produced and bottled.

SPICES

Spices contribute an additional layer of flavor to many of the biscotti in this book. In general, whole spices keep longer than ground spices. I have a small nutmeg grater that I use to grate whole nutmeg. Be sure to use ground spices that have not lost their potency. A good way to tell is to shake the jar (with the cap still on), wait a moment, and then open the jar and sniff to see how strong the aroma is. If it's faint, it's time to get a new jar.

VIN SANTO

This sweet (or sometimes dry) dessert wine is produced in several regions in Italy but is mostly associated with Tuscany. It is made from late-harvest grapes that are air-dried before being pressed. The fermented juice is aged for three to five years in small barrels, traditionally made from chestnut but now made mostly from oak. It is *the* beverage to sip while eating classic cantucci.

TECHNIQUES

It's not difficult to master the techniques to make perfect biscotti—mixing and shaping the dough, slicing the baked logs, toasting nuts, melting chocolate, and so on. Read through this section to familiarize yourself with the techniques used throughout this book. As with any cooking or baking process, the more you do it, the more accomplished you become.

PREPPING NUTS
Many recipes in this book call for toasting nuts or removing their skins, or both. Follow these simple instructions to remove the skins from almonds, hazelnuts, and pistachios.

ALMONDS: Place raw, skin-on almonds in a heat-proof bowl and pour boiling water over them. Let sit about 1 minute to loosen the skins. Drain and rinse, and use your fingers to pop the almonds out of their skins.

HAZELNUTS: Heat the oven to 350°F/180°C. Spread the shelled nuts on a rimmed baking sheet and bake for 10 minutes, or until the skins have begun to crackle. Wrap the hot hazelnuts in a clean kitchen towel and let stand about 1 minute. Roll the nuts back and forth in the towel to loosen and rub off the skins. Not all the skins will come off, which is fine.

PISTACHIOS: Place the nuts in a heat-proof bowl and pour enough boiling water over them to cover. Let sit for 2 minutes and then drain. You can either slip the skins off with your fingers or wrap the nuts in a clean kitchen towel and roll them back and forth to remove the skins. I find the towel method removes some of the skins but not all, so I use my fingers.

TOASTING NUTS
Heat the oven to 350°F/180°C. Spread the shelled nuts on a rimmed baking sheet and bake for 7 to 10 minutes, until they are fragrant.

TOASTING COCONUT
Heat the oven to 325°F/160°C. Spread the flakes on a rimmed baking sheet and bake, stirring once or twice, for 3 to 5 minutes, or until the flakes are lightly browned. Keep a close watch, as coconut can quickly go from browned to burned.

TOASTING FENNEL SEEDS
Spread the seeds in a dry heavy skillet and set over medium-high heat. Gently shake the skillet or stir the spices with a heat-proof spatula to move them around as the skillet heats. Cook for 3 to 5 minutes, just until the seeds have turned a shade darker and are fragrant.

MEASURING FLOUR
The most accurate way to measure flour is by weight in grams. Use a digital scale

with a metric setting if you have one. If you don't and are measuring by the cup, lightly spoon the flour into a measuring cup until it is overflowing and then sweep across the top with the flat edge of a knife or metal spatula to level. Do this over a piece of wax paper to catch the excess flour.

MELTING CHOCOLATE

To melt bittersweet, semisweet, or milk chocolate, chop coarsely and put the pieces in the top of a double boiler set over (but not touching) barely simmering water. Or put the pieces in a heat-proof bowl and set the bowl over (but not touching) a pan of barely simmering water. Heat, stirring gently, until the chocolate is melted and smooth. To melt in the microwave, put the pieces of chocolate in a microwave-proof bowl and microwave at 50 percent power in 30-second intervals until melted and smooth. Stir after each interval.

MIXING BISCOTTI DOUGH

The traditional method is the same one used to make fresh pasta. That is, you mound your dry ingredients on a counter-top, make a well in the center, add in your eggs and other "wet" ingredients, and gradually incorporate the wet into the dry until a dough is formed. However, modern convenience has given us the stand mixer, which I find works just as well. I fit my stand mixer with the flat paddle attachment, which I prefer to the whisk attachment because it mixes the ingredients without incorporating too much air. It also does a good job of breaking up nuts, but not too finely. You can use a food processor, again starting with dry ingredients and adding in the wet ones. However, I find the blade tends to chop the nuts too finely.

CHILLING THE DOUGH

This is optional, done mostly for convenience. You can chill it for as little as an hour or as long as overnight. Because biscotti dough is often soft and sticky, refrigerating it until firm makes it easier to handle and shape into logs. Generally, though, I like to shape the dough right after mixing it and get on with the baking.

SHAPING THE DOUGH

The soft, tacky dough can be tricky to handle, as it has a tendency to cake on your fingers. It can be difficult to roll out into a log shape and cumbersome to transfer to the oiled baking sheet. After trying a number of different methods, I settled on this one, which is not especially elegant but is easy and works beautifully. Place the dough on a lightly floured countertop and divide it according to the recipe instructions.

Lightly moisten your hands, either with a tiny bit of water or with vegetable oil. Shape a portion of dough into a rough oval and, with moistened hands, transfer it to the prepared baking sheet. Then use your hands and fingers to gently stretch and pat the dough into a log shape.

The size of the log will depend on the recipe. Some recipes call for wide logs, to yield bigger biscotti. Some recipes call for dividing the dough into three or four portions to yield smaller logs to make smaller biscotti. Of course, you can make the biscotti any size you prefer (see more about this under "Slicing the Logs," at right).

USING EGG WASH

Most traditional recipes for classic cantucci call for brushing the log of dough with beaten egg before baking. This creates a glossy surface. I have kept this step in a few of the more traditional recipes in the book. But in most of the recipes I omitted it because I happen to like the more rustic nonglossy look.

BAKING THE LOGS

All of the recipes call for baking the logs of dough at 350°F/180°C. Once sliced, the biscotti are returned to the oven at a lower heat—300° to 325°F/150° to 165°C—for a second baking, the purpose of which is to dry them out without browning them too much. The biscotti made without butter or oil become crunchy during this second baking, while those that contain a little fat tend to be crispy and a little more delicate in texture. Keep in mind that the biscotti will get crunchier as they cool.

In general, it takes 25 minutes for an uncut log to bake. You can tell when it's done by pressing lightly on the top—it should spring back and there should be cracks on the surface. After slicing, the second baking can take anywhere from 8 to 20 minutes per side, depending on whether there is fat in the dough, how thickly you slice the log, and how hot the oven is.

SLICING THE LOGS

After the first baking, the logs are sliced on the diagonal to make that classic angled biscotti shape. The more acute the angle of your knife, the longer your slices will be. And (obviously) the thicker the slice, the fatter your biscotti will be. I sliced the biscotti in these recipes according to how I wanted the finished cookies to look and how big or small I wanted them to be. For example, I sliced the Cappuccino Dunkers (page 90) on an acute angle to create long cookies perfect for dunking. But for the Sun-Dried Tomato and Fennel biscotti (page 122), I made thin logs, which I then cut into fat slices to make two-bite savory cookies that are the perfect appetizer size.

For years, I used a serrated bread knife to gently saw the baked logs into slices. Although this works fairly well, pieces of nuts can snag on the knife's teeth, which causes the occasional cookie to crumble or break. Still, it works better than a chef's knife, which has a tendency to compress and flatten the slices. But I recently found a better way. I was at a farmers' market in Glen Arbor, Michigan, where I met a woman selling homemade biscotti. We got to talking and she mentioned she uses a Santoku knife—a Japanese knife with a flat-edge blade. This, I found, works beautifully. No sawing required. Just press down and cut as though you were slicing an onion. The Santoku slices through the log without compressing it. So a tip of the hat to that Michigan baker who shared her secret. If you don't have a Santoku, use a serrated bread knife.

ICING BISCOTTI

A number of recipes call for dipping biscotti in melted chocolate or for drizzling melted chocolate or a sugar-based icing over them. Follow the instructions on page 17 for melting chocolate. To minimize mess, I line a rimmed baking sheet with wax paper or parchment paper and set a cooling rack over it. You can either lay your biscotti on their sides or stand them upright. To drizzle, dip a fork or the tip of a whisk into the icing (or melted chocolate) and wave it back and forth over the cookies. Chill the biscotti briefly in the refrigerator to set the icing.

STORING BISCOTTI

Most biscotti last at least a week. Those made without butter or oil last longer, at least two weeks. To keep them crisp, store biscotti in metal containers with tight-fitting lids at room temperature. I don't recommend refrigerating or freezing biscotti, as they tend to lose their crunch when defrosted.

CLASSIC FLAVORS

ALMOND

★

1 TBSP VEGETABLE OIL

2 CUPS/255 G
UNBLEACHED
ALL-PURPOSE FLOUR

1 CUP/200 G SUGAR,
PLUS 2 TBSP

½ TSP BAKING POWDER

¼ TSP FINE SEA SALT

SCANT 1 CUP/125 G
BLANCHED (PEELED)
WHOLE ALMONDS, LIGHTLY
TOASTED (SEE PAGE 16),
AND HALVED

3 LARGE EGGS;
1 SEPARATED

1 TSP PURE ALMOND
EXTRACT

½ TSP PURE VANILLA
EXTRACT

MAKES **40** TO **42** BISCOTTI

Here is my version of the "original" biscotti recipe—or cantucci di Prato, as they are referred to in Italy. They are satisfyingly crunchy and infused with delicate almond flavor.

Heat the oven to 350°F/180°C. Lightly coat an 11-by-17-in/28-by-43-cm rimmed baking sheet with the oil.

Combine the flour, 1 cup/200 g sugar, baking powder, and salt in the bowl of a stand mixer fitted with the paddle attachment. Add the almonds and mix on low speed to combine. Lightly beat the eggs and egg yolk, add to the bowl with the almond extract and vanilla, and mix on medium speed until a soft, slightly sticky dough has formed.

Turn the dough out onto a lightly floured work surface and pat it into a disk. Divide it into quarters. Lightly moisten your hands with water and gently roll one portion of dough into a rough oval. Place it crosswise on the prepared baking sheet and use your hands and fingers to stretch and pat the dough into a log about 1½ in/4 cm wide and 9 in/23 cm long. Shape the remaining pieces of dough in the same way, moistening your hands as necessary, leaving at least 2 in/5 cm between the logs. Press down on the logs to flatten them out a bit and make the tops even. Lightly beat the egg white and brush it over the tops of the logs. Sprinkle the remaining 2 Tbsp sugar over the tops of the logs.

Bake the logs for 20 to 25 minutes, or until they are lightly browned and just set—they should be springy to the touch and there should be cracks on the surface. Transfer the baking sheet to a cooling rack. Gently slide an offset spatula under each log to loosen it from the baking sheet. Let the logs cool for 5 minutes,

CONT'D

and then transfer them to the rack and let cool for 20 minutes. Lower the oven temperature to 300°F/150°C.

Transfer the cooled logs, one at a time, to a cutting board and, using a Santoku knife or a serrated bread knife, cut them on the diagonal into ¾-in-/2-cm-thick slices. Arrange the slices, cut-side up, on the baking sheet (in batches if necessary) and bake for 10 minutes. Turn the slices over and bake for another 10 minutes, until they are crisp. Transfer the slices to the rack to cool completely. The biscotti will keep for up to 2 weeks in an airtight container stored at room temperature.

WHAT TO DRINK: Vin Santo, the traditional Tuscan dessert wine.

HAZELNUT

This riff on traditional almond cantucci stars toasty hazelnuts in place of the almonds. Their flavor is slightly more robust than classic almond cantucci. I especially like to make these in fall, with freshly harvested hazelnuts from Oregon, if I can find them.

Heat the oven to 350°F/180°C. Lightly coat an 11-by-17-in/ 28-by-43-cm rimmed baking sheet with the vegetable oil.

Combine the flour, sugar, baking powder, and salt in the bowl of a stand mixer fitted with the paddle attachment. Add the hazelnuts and mix on low speed to combine and break up some of the nuts. Add the eggs, hazelnut oil, vanilla, and orange extract (if using) and mix on medium speed until a soft, slightly sticky dough has formed.

Turn the dough out onto a lightly floured work surface and pat it into a disk. Divide it into quarters. Lightly moisten your hands with water and gently roll one portion of dough into a rough oval. Place it crosswise on the prepared baking sheet and use your hands and fingers to stretch and pat the dough into a log about 1½ in/4 cm wide and 9 in/23 cm long. Shape the remaining pieces of dough in the same way, moistening your hands as necessary, leaving at least 2 in/5 cm between the logs. Press down on the logs to flatten them out a bit and make the tops even.

Bake the logs for 20 to 25 minutes, or until they are lightly browned and just set—they should be springy to the touch and there should be cracks on the surface. Transfer the baking sheet to a cooling rack. Gently slide an offset spatula under each log to loosen it from the baking sheet. Let the logs cool for 5 minutes, and then transfer them to the rack and let cool for 20 minutes. Lower the oven temperature to 325°F/165°C.

★

1 TBSP VEGETABLE OIL

2 CUPS/255 G UNBLEACHED ALL-PURPOSE FLOUR

1 CUP/200 G SUGAR

½ TSP BAKING POWDER

¼ TSP FINE SEA SALT

¾ CUP/105 G HAZELNUTS, TOASTED (SEE PAGE 16) AND SKINNED

2 LARGE EGGS, LIGHTLY BEATEN

2 TBSP HAZELNUT OIL OR EXTRA-VIRGIN OLIVE OIL

1 TSP PURE VANILLA EXTRACT

½ TSP PURE ORANGE EXTRACT (OPTIONAL)

MAKES **40** TO **42** BISCOTTI

CONT'D

Transfer the cooled logs, one at a time, to a cutting board and, using a Santoku knife or a serrated bread knife, cut them on the diagonal into ¾-in-/2-cm-thick slices. Arrange the slices, cut-side up, on the baking sheet (in batches if necessary) and bake for 10 minutes. Turn the slices over and bake for another 10 minutes, until they are crisp. Transfer the slices to the rack to cool completely. The biscotti will keep for up to 2 weeks in an airtight container stored at room temperature.

WHAT TO DRINK: Luxardo Angioletto, a traditional toasted hazelnut liqueur, or a glass of sherry. These would also be delicious with an espresso.

VIN SANTO

WITH ALMONDS AND HAZELNUTS

★

- 1 TBSP VEGETABLE OIL

- 2 CUPS/255 G UNBLEACHED ALL-PURPOSE FLOUR

- 1 CUP/200 G SUGAR

- ½ TSP BAKING POWDER

- ¼ TSP FINE SEA SALT

- ½ CUP/70 G WHOLE ALMONDS, TOASTED (SEE PAGE 16)

- ¼ CUP/35 G HAZELNUTS, TOASTED (SEE PAGE 16) AND SKINNED

- 2 LARGE EGGS, LIGHTLY BEATEN

- 2 TBSP VIN SANTO (SEE PAGE 15)

- 1 TSP PURE VANILLA EXTRACT

MAKES **40** TO **42** BISCOTTI

Since classic cantucci are traditionally served with a glass of Vin Santo, it only made sense to me to try adding a splash of the dessert wine to the cookie dough itself. It was a good call; the sweet wine rounds out the flavor of the cookies nicely and makes them, in my opinion, all the more dunkable.

Heat the oven to 350°F/180°C. Lightly coat an 11-by-17-in/ 28-by-43-cm rimmed baking sheet with the oil.

Combine the flour, sugar, baking powder, and salt in the bowl of a stand mixer fitted with the paddle attachment. Mix briefly on low speed. Add the almonds and hazelnuts and mix on low to combine and break up some of the nuts.

Set aside 1 Tbsp of the beaten eggs. Add the remaining eggs, Vin Santo, and vanilla to the dry ingredients and mix on medium speed until a soft, slightly sticky dough has formed.

Turn the dough out onto a lightly floured work surface and pat it into a disk. Divide it into quarters. Lightly moisten your hands with water and gently roll one portion of dough into a rough oval. Place it crosswise on the prepared baking sheet and use your hands and fingers to stretch and pat the dough into a log about 1½ in/4 cm wide and 9 in/23 cm long. Shape the remaining pieces of dough in the same way, moistening your hands as necessary, leaving at least 2 in/5 cm between the logs. Press down on the logs to flatten them out a bit and make the tops even. Brush the tops with the reserved beaten egg.

Bake the logs for 20 to 25 minutes, or until they are lightly browned and just set—they should be springy to the touch and there should be cracks on the surface. Transfer the baking sheet to a cooling rack. Gently slide an offset spatula under each log to loosen it from the baking sheet. Let the logs cool for 5 minutes, and then transfer them to the rack and let cool for 20 minutes. Lower the oven temperature to 325°F/165°C.

Transfer the cooled logs, one at a time, to a cutting board and, using a Santoku knife or a serrated bread knife, cut them on the diagonal into ¾-in-/2-cm-thick slices. Arrange the slices, cut-side up, on the baking sheet (in batches if necessary) and bake for 10 minutes. Turn the slices over and bake for another 10 minutes, until they are crisp. Transfer the slices to the rack to cool completely. The biscotti will keep for up to 2 weeks in an airtight container stored at room temperature.

WHAT TO DRINK: Vin Santo, of course.

ANISE

1 TBSP VEGETABLE OIL

2 CUPS/255 G
UNBLEACHED
ALL-PURPOSE FLOUR

1 CUP/200 G SUGAR,
PLUS 2 TBSP

½ TSP BAKING POWDER

⅛ TSP SALT

1 TBSP ANISEED

SCANT 1 CUP/125 G
WHOLE ALMONDS, TOASTED
(SEE PAGE 16)

3 LARGE EGGS;
1 SEPARATED

2 TBSP SAMBUCA OR
OTHER ANISE-FLAVORED
LIQUEUR

MAKES ABOUT 34 BISCOTTI

Count me among the anise lovers of the world. Its herbaceous licorice flavor reminds me of festivals and holidays, which is when you'll find anise-spiked cookies on many Italian cookie plates. You don't need a special occasion to enjoy these crunchy cookies.

Heat the oven to 350°F/180°C. Lightly coat an 11-by-17-in/ 28-by-43-cm rimmed baking sheet with the oil.

Combine the flour, 1 cup/200 g sugar, baking powder, salt, and aniseed in the bowl of a stand mixer fitted with the paddle attachment. Mix briefly on low speed. Add the almonds and mix on low to combine. Lightly beat the eggs and egg yolk, add to the bowl with the sambuca, and mix on medium speed until a soft, slightly sticky dough has formed.

Turn the dough out onto a lightly floured work surface and pat it into a disk. Divide it into three equal pieces. Lightly moisten your hands with water and gently roll one portion of dough into a rough oval. Place it crosswise on the prepared baking sheet and use your hands and fingers to stretch and pat the dough into a log about 2 in/5 cm wide and 10 in/25 cm long. Shape the remaining pieces of dough in the same way, moistening your hands as necessary, leaving at least 2 in/5 cm between the logs. Press down on the logs to flatten them out a bit and make the tops even. Lightly beat the reserved egg white and brush it over the tops of the logs. Sprinkle the remaining 2 Tbsp sugar over the tops of the logs.

Bake the logs for 20 to 25 minutes, or until they are lightly browned and just set—they should be springy to the touch and there should be cracks on the surface. Transfer the baking sheet to a cooling rack. Gently slide an offset spatula under each log to loosen it from the baking sheet. Let the logs cool for 5 minutes, and then transfer them to the rack and let cool for 20 minutes. Lower the oven temperature to 300°F/150°C.

Transfer the cooled logs, one at a time, to a cutting board and, using a Santoku knife or a serrated bread knife, cut them on the diagonal into ¾-in-/2-cm-thick slices. Arrange the slices, cut-side up, on the baking sheet (in batches if necessary) and bake for 10 minutes. Turn the slices over and bake for another 10 minutes, until they are crisp. Transfer the slices to the rack to cool completely. The biscotti will keep for up to 2 weeks in an airtight container stored at room temperature.

WHAT TO DRINK: An anise-flavored liqueur such as sambuca or Pernod.

LEMON

★

1 TBSP VEGETABLE OIL

2 CUPS/255 G
UNBLEACHED
ALL-PURPOSE FLOUR

1¼ CUPS/250 G SUGAR

½ TSP BAKING POWDER

⅛ TSP FINE SEA SALT

SCANT 1 CUP/125 G
WHOLE ALMONDS, TOASTED
(SEE PAGE 16)

3 LARGE EGGS:
1 SEPARATED

½ TSP PURE VANILLA
EXTRACT

¼ TSP PURE LEMON
EXTRACT

MAKES ABOUT 30 BISCOTTI

This is the first biscotti recipe that I dreamed up on my own. I was going for something crunchy and classic, but with just a little bit more flavor than basic almond biscotti. Pure lemon extract became my "little bit more." If you can't find pure lemon extract, you can substitute lemon essence, or even a squeeze of lemon juice and some finely grated zest.

Heat the oven to 350°F/180°C. Lightly coat an 11-by-17-in/28-by-43-cm rimmed baking sheet with the oil.

Combine the flour, sugar, baking powder, and salt in the bowl of a stand mixer fitted with the paddle attachment. Add the almonds and mix on low speed to combine and break up some of the almonds. Lightly beat the eggs and egg yolk and add them to the bowl with the vanilla and lemon extract. Mix on medium speed until a soft, slightly sticky dough has formed.

Turn the dough out onto a lightly floured work surface and pat it into a disk. Divide it in half. Lightly moisten your hands with water and gently roll one portion of dough into a rough oval. Place it lengthwise on one half of the baking sheet and use your hands and fingers to stretch and pat the dough into a log about 2½ in/6 cm wide and 12 in/30 cm long. Shape the second piece of dough in the same way, moistening your hands as necessary. Press down on the logs to flatten them out a bit and make the tops even. Lightly beat the reserved egg white and brush it over the tops of the logs.

Bake the logs for 25 minutes, or until they are lightly browned and just set—they should be springy to the touch and there should be cracks on the surface. Transfer the baking sheet to a cooling rack. Gently slide an offset spatula under each log to loosen it from the baking sheet. Let the logs cool for 5 minutes, and then transfer them to the rack and let cool for 20 minutes. Lower the oven temperature to 325°F/165°C.

Transfer the cooled logs, one at a time, to a cutting board and, using a Santoku knife or a serrated bread knife, cut them on the diagonal into ¾-in-/2-cm-thick slices. Arrange the slices, cut-side up, on the baking sheet (in batches if necessary) and bake for 10 minutes. Turn the slices over and bake for another 10 minutes, until they are crisp. Transfer the slices to the rack to cool completely. The biscotti will keep for up to 2 weeks in an airtight container stored at room temperature.

WHAT TO DRINK: Lemon-flavored liqueur such as limoncello or crema di limoncello.

HONEY-ALMOND

1 TBSP VEGETABLE OIL

1¾ CUPS/185 G
UNBLEACHED
ALL-PURPOSE FLOUR

¼ CUP/25 G ALMOND
FLOUR OR ALMOND
MEAL (SEE PAGE 14)

½ TSP BAKING POWDER

¼ TSP FINE SEA SALT

2 LARGE EGGS, SEPARATED

1 TBSP HONEY

½ TSP PURE ALMOND
EXTRACT

¾ CUP/150 G SUGAR

¾ CUP/105 G WHOLE
ALMONDS, TOASTED
(SEE PAGE 16) AND
HALVED CROSSWISE

MAKES ABOUT 40 BISCOTTI

This recipe is only slightly different from the basic almond cantucci, but the difference is noticeable. Whipping the egg whites produces biscotti that are slightly airier in texture. A touch of honey and almond extract deepens the cookies' flavor. If I had to choose between classic cantucci and these, I'd be tempted to pick these.

Heat the oven to 350°F/180°C. Lightly coat an 11-by-17-in/ 28-by-43-cm rimmed baking sheet with the oil.

Combine the all-purpose flour, almond flour, baking powder, and salt in a medium bowl and whisk until well incorporated. In a small bowl, whisk the egg yolks with the honey and almond extract. Set both bowls aside.

In a stand mixer fitted with the whisk attachment, beat the egg whites until foamy. Gradually beat in the sugar and continue beating until the egg whites are thick, glossy, and sticky, like marshmallow spread. Pour the egg yolk mixture into the egg white mixture and beat until combined, scraping down the sides of the mixer bowl as needed. Switch the whisk attachment to the paddle attachment. Dump the flour mixture into the egg mixture and beat on low speed until just combined. Add the toasted almonds and mix on low until a soft, sticky dough has formed.

Turn the dough out onto a lightly floured work surface and pat it into a disk. Divide it in half. Lightly moisten your hands with water and gently roll one portion of dough into a rough oval. Place it lengthwise on one half of the baking sheet and use your hands and fingers to stretch and pat the dough into a log about 2½ in/6 cm wide and 12 in/30 cm long. Shape the second piece of dough in the same way, moistening your hands as necessary. Press down on the logs to flatten them out a bit and make the tops even.

Bake the logs for 20 minutes, or until they are lightly browned and just set—they should be springy to the touch and there should be cracks on the surface. Transfer the baking sheet to a cooling rack. Gently slide an offset spatula under each log to loosen it from the baking sheet. Let the logs cool for 5 minutes, and then transfer them to the rack and let cool for 20 minutes. Lower the oven temperature to 300°F/150°C.

Transfer the cooled logs to a cutting board and, using a Santoku knife or a serrated bread knife, cut them on the diagonal into ½-in-/12-mm-thick slices. Arrange the slices, cut-side up, on the baking sheet (in batches if necessary) and bake for 8 minutes. Turn the slices over and bake for another 8 minutes, or until they are crisp. Transfer the slices to the rack to cool completely. The biscotti will keep for up to 2 weeks in an airtight container stored at room temperature.

WHAT TO DRINK: Amaretto, a sweet, almond-flavored liqueur.

OLIVE OIL

AND

CITRUS

1 TBSP VEGETABLE OIL

2 CUPS/255 G
UNBLEACHED
ALL-PURPOSE FLOUR

1 TBSP POLENTA (COARSE
CORNMEAL)

1 TSP BAKING POWDER

⅛ TSP FINE SEA SALT

¾ CUP/150 G FIRMLY
PACKED LIGHT BROWN
SUGAR

¾ CUP/75 G SLICED
ALMONDS

1 TO 2 TSP ANISEED

The warm, sweet aromas of Sicily—orange, lemon, and spicy anise—are baked right into these biscotti. Adding olive oil enriches the dough and yields a cookie that is slightly less crunchy than the Almond biscotti (page 22), but it is still crisp and can definitely stand up to a good dunk!

Heat the oven to 350°F/180°C. Lightly coat an 11-by-17-in/ 28-by-43-cm rimmed baking sheet with the vegetable oil.

Combine the flour, polenta, baking powder, salt, and brown sugar in the bowl of a stand mixer fitted with the paddle attachment. Mix briefly on low speed. Add the almonds, aniseed, orange zest, and lemon zest and mix briefly on low to combine. With the motor running, drizzle in the olive oil and lemon extract. Lightly beat the eggs and egg yolk and add to the bowl. Mix on medium speed until a soft, slightly sticky dough has formed.

Turn the dough out onto a lightly floured work surface and pat it into a disk. Divide it in half. Lightly moisten your hands with water and gently roll one portion of dough into a rough oval. Place it lengthwise on one half of the baking sheet and use your hands and fingers to stretch and pat the dough into a log about 2½ in/6 cm wide and 12 in/30 cm long. Shape the second piece of dough in the same way, moistening your hands as necessary. Press down on the logs to flatten them out a bit and make the tops even. Lightly beat the egg white and brush it over the tops of the logs.

Bake the logs for 25 minutes, or until they are lightly browned and just set—they should be springy to the touch and there should be cracks on the surface. Transfer the baking sheet to a cooling rack. Gently slide an offset spatula under each log to loosen it from the baking sheet. Let the logs cool for 5 minutes, and then transfer them to the rack and let cool for 20 minutes. Lower the oven temperature to 325°F/165°C.

Transfer the cooled logs to a cutting board and, using a Santoku knife or a serrated bread knife, cut them on the diagonal into ¾-in-/2-cm-thick slices. Arrange the slices, cut-side up, on the baking sheet (in batches if necessary) and bake for 10 minutes. Turn the slices over and bake for another 10 minutes, until they are crisp. Transfer the slices to the rack to cool completely. The biscotti will keep for up to 10 days in an airtight container stored at room temperature.

WHAT TO DRINK: A cup of chamomile tea.

★

FINELY GRATED ZEST OF
1 ORGANIC ORANGE

FINELY GRATED ZEST OF
1 ORGANIC LEMON

6 TBSP EXTRA-VIRGIN
OLIVE OIL

½ TSP PURE LEMON
EXTRACT

3 LARGE EGGS;
1 SEPARATED

MAKES ABOUT BISCOTTI

ORANGE

AND

PISTACHIO

★

1 TBSP VEGETABLE OIL

2 CUPS/255 G
UNBLEACHED
ALL-PURPOSE FLOUR

½ TSP BAKING POWDER

¼ TSP FINE SEA SALT

2 LARGE EGGS, SEPARATED

1 TBSP HONEY

1 TBSP PISTACHIO OIL OR
EXTRA-VIRGIN OLIVE OIL

1 TSP PURE ORANGE
EXTRACT

FINELY GRATED ZEST OF
1 ORGANIC ORANGE

¾ CUP/150 G SUGAR

1 CUP/120 G SHELLED
ROASTED UNSALTED
PISTACHIOS

MAKES ABOUT 40 BISCOTTI

My original idea for these sweetly perfumed cookies was to create a biscotto with a splash of orange-flower water in the dough. But when I opened the bottle of orange-flower water I'd bought, I found it was way too flowery for my taste. So I chose the more conventional orange extract. Adding 1 Tbsp of pistachio oil to the dough enriches the earthy flavor of the nuts, but if you don't have any on hand or don't care to buy it, you can use olive oil. The cookies will still be delicious.

Heat the oven to 350°F/180°C. Lightly coat an 11-by-17-in/ 28-by-43-cm rimmed baking sheet with the vegetable oil.

Combine the flour, baking powder, and salt in a medium bowl and whisk until well incorporated. In a small bowl, whisk the egg yolks with the honey, pistachio oil, orange extract, and orange zest. Set both bowls aside.

In a stand mixer fitted with the whisk attachment, beat the egg whites until foamy. Gradually beat in the sugar and continue beating until the egg whites are thick, glossy, and sticky, like marshmallow spread. Pour the egg yolk mixture into the egg white mixture and beat until combined, scraping down the sides of the mixer bowl as needed. Switch the whisk attachment to the paddle attachment. Dump the flour mixture into the egg mixture and beat on low speed until just combined. Add the pistachios and mix on low until a soft, sticky dough has formed.

CONT'D

ARANCIA

Turn the dough out onto a lightly floured work surface and pat it into a disk. Divide it in half. Lightly moisten your hands with water and gently roll one portion of dough into a rough oval. Place it lengthwise on one half of the baking sheet and use your hands and fingers to stretch and pat the dough into a log about 2½ in/6 cm wide and 12 in/30 cm long. Shape the second piece of dough in the same way, moistening your hands as necessary. Press down on the logs to flatten them out a bit and make the tops even.

Bake the logs for 20 minutes, or until they are lightly browned and just set—they should be springy to the touch and there should be cracks on the surface. Transfer the baking sheet to a cooling rack. Gently slide an offset spatula under each log to loosen it from the baking sheet. Let the logs cool for 5 minutes, and then transfer them to the rack and let cool for 20 minutes. Lower the oven temperature to 300°F/150°C.

Transfer the cooled logs to a cutting board and, using a Santoku knife or a serrated bread knife, cut them on the diagonal into ½-in-/12-mm-thick slices. Arrange the slices, cut-side up, on the baking sheet (in batches if necessary) and bake for 8 minutes. Carefully turn the slices over and bake for another 8 minutes, or until they are crisp. Transfer the slices to the rack to cool completely. The biscotti will keep for up to 10 days in an airtight container stored at room temperature.

WHAT TO DRINK: Aperol Spritz, a refreshing cocktail made with Aperol and Prosecco, garnished with an orange slice.

FIG

These extra-large slices are loaded with warm, toasty hazelnuts and chunks of sweet fig. Strictly speaking, these aren't true biscotti, as they are baked only once. This keeps them chewy-soft and prevents the dried fruit from toughening. Look for Calimyrna figs, which are lighter in color than black Mission figs. Dried Calimyrnas also tend to be softer and plumper, and they have a sweet, caramel-like flavor.

Heat the oven to 350°F/180°C. Lightly coat an 11-by-17-in/ 28-by-43-cm rimmed baking sheet with the vegetable oil.

Combine the flour, sugar, baking powder, and salt in the bowl of a stand mixer fitted with the paddle attachment. Add the hazelnuts, figs, and lemon zest and mix on low speed to combine and break up some of the nuts. Add the eggs, honey, and olive oil and mix on medium speed until a soft, sticky dough has formed.

Turn the dough out onto a lightly floured work surface and pat it into a disk. Lightly moisten your hands with water and gently roll the dough into a rough oval. Place it lengthwise in the middle of the baking sheet and use your hands and fingers to stretch and pat the dough into a log about 3½ in/9 cm wide and 14 in/35 cm long. Press down on the log to flatten it out a bit and make the top even.

Bake the log for 25 to 30 minutes, or until it is lightly browned and just set—it should be springy to the touch and

CONT'D

★

1 TBSP VEGETABLE OIL

2 CUPS/255 G
UNBLEACHED
ALL-PURPOSE FLOUR

½ CUP/100 G SUGAR

1 TSP BAKING POWDER

⅛ TSP FINE SEA SALT

1 CUP/140 G HAZELNUTS,
TOASTED (SEE PAGE 16)
AND SKINNED

SCANT 1 CUP/140 G
DRIED CALIMYRNA FIGS,
QUARTERED

FINELY GRATED ZEST OF
1 ORGANIC LEMON

2 LARGE EGGS,
LIGHTLY BEATEN

2 TBSP HONEY

2 TBSP EXTRA-VIRGIN
OLIVE OIL

MAKES
18 TO 20
LARGE BISCOTTI

there should be cracks on the surface. Transfer the baking sheet to a cooling rack. Gently slide an offset spatula under the log to loosen it from the baking sheet. Let the log cool for 5 minutes, and then transfer it to the rack and let it cool to room temperature.

Transfer the cooled log to a cutting board and, using a Santoku knife or a serrated bread knife, cut it on the diagonal into ⅜-in-/1-cm-thick slices. These are best enjoyed on the day they are made, though they will keep in an airtight container stored at room temperature for up to 3 days.

WHAT TO DRINK: A glass of port or cider, hot or cold.

CHOCOLATE
AND
SPICE

CHOCOLATE KISSES

1 TBSP VEGETABLE OIL

2 CUPS/255 G
UNBLEACHED
ALL-PURPOSE FLOUR

¾ CUP/150 G SUGAR

¼ CUP/20 G UNSWEETENED
COCOA POWDER

1 TSP BAKING POWDER

¼ TSP FINE SEA SALT

¾ CUP/105 G HAZELNUTS,
TOASTED AND SKINNED
(SEE PAGE 16),
COARSELY CHOPPED

6 TBSP/85 G UNSALTED
BUTTER, CUT INTO
½-IN/12-MM PIECES, AT
COOL ROOM TEMPERATURE

2 LARGE EGGS,
LIGHTLY BEATEN

As a kid I loved Baci, those hazelnut-crowned chocolate "kisses" wrapped in their trademark blue-and-silver foil. The silhouette of the embracing couple on the candy box seemed so darkly romantic—verging on forbidden—to my child's mind, as did the mysterious love messages in tiny print on the slips of waxy paper tucked inside the wrapper. I still love the bittersweet combination of dark chocolate and hazelnuts, and that is exactly what you get with these biscotti. Deeply chocolaty, not too sweet. Slightly mysterious.

Heat the oven to 350°F/180°C. Lightly coat an 11-by-17-in/ 28-by-43-cm rimmed baking sheet with the oil.

Combine the flour, sugar, cocoa powder, baking powder, and salt in the bowl of a stand mixer fitted with the paddle attachment. Mix briefly on low speed. Add the hazelnuts and mix briefly on low to combine. Add the butter in pieces and mix until incorporated. Pour in the eggs and mix on medium-low speed until the mixture begins to come together.

Whisk together the melted chocolate and espresso powder. Scrape the mixture into the flour-egg mixture and mix just until incorporated. Add the bittersweet chocolate pieces and mix on medium-low speed until a soft, slightly sticky dough has formed.

Turn the dough out onto a lightly floured work surface and pat it into a disk. Divide it in half. Lightly moisten your hands with water and gently roll one portion of dough into a rough oval. Place it lengthwise on one half the baking sheet and use your hands and fingers to stretch and pat the dough into a log about 2½ in/6 cm wide and 11 to 12 in/28 to 30 cm long. Shape the second piece of dough in the same way, moistening your hands as necessary. Press down on the logs to flatten them out a bit and make the tops even.

Bake the logs for 25 minutes, or until they are just set—they should be springy to the touch and there should be cracks on the surface. Transfer the baking sheet to a cooling rack. Gently slide an offset spatula under each log to loosen it from the baking sheet. Let the logs cool on the sheet for 5 minutes, and then transfer them to the rack and let cool for 20 minutes. Lower the oven temperature to 325°F/165°C.

Transfer the cooled logs to a cutting board and, using a Santoku knife or a serrated bread knife, cut them on the diagonal into ½-in-/12-mm-thick slices. Arrange the slices, cut-side up, on the baking sheet (in batches if necessary) and bake for 10 minutes. Turn the slices over and bake for another 10 minutes, until they are crisp. Transfer the slices to the rack to cool completely. The biscotti will keep for up to 2 weeks in an airtight container stored at room temperature.

WHAT TO DRINK: A shot of extra-strong espresso.

★

4 OZ/115 G UNSWEETENED CHOCOLATE, MELTED (SEE PAGE 17) AND COOLED SLIGHTLY

1 TBSP INSTANT ESPRESSO POWDER

3 OZ/85 G BITTERSWEET CHOCOLATE, CUT INTO SMALL PIECES

MAKES ABOUT 40 BISCOTTI

CHOCOLATE-ALMOND

WITH PISTACHIOS

★

1 TBSP VEGETABLE OIL

½ CUP/70 G BLANCHED
(PEELED) WHOLE ALMONDS

¾ CUP/150 G SUGAR

2 CUPS/255 G
UNBLEACHED
ALL-PURPOSE FLOUR

2 TBSP UNSWEETENED
COCOA POWDER

1 TSP BAKING POWDER

¼ TSP FINE SEA SALT

⅔ CUP/85 G SHELLED
UNSALTED ROASTED
PISTACHIOS

6 TBSP/85 G UNSALTED
BUTTER, CUT INTO
½-IN/12-MM PIECES, AT
COOL ROOM TEMPERATURE

I can't say that these rich cookies are authentically Sicilian. However, I think of them as Sicilian in spirit because they feature ingredients found in many Sicilian sweets: good bittersweet chocolate, pulverized almonds, and rich pistachios.

Heat the oven to 350°F/180°C. Lightly coat an 11-by-17-in/ 28-by-43-cm rimmed baking sheet with the oil.

Combine the almonds and sugar in the work bowl of a food processor fitted with the metal blade. Process until the almonds are very finely ground but not so fine that they begin to turn into a paste. Transfer the pulverized almonds and sugar to the bowl of a stand mixer fitted with the paddle attachment. Add the flour, cocoa powder, baking powder, and salt and mix briefly on low speed. Add the pistachios and mix briefly on low to combine. Add the butter in pieces and mix on medium-low speed until the mixture looks like damp sand. Add the eggs and almond extract and mix briefly. Scrape in the melted chocolate and mix on medium speed until a soft, slightly sticky dough has formed.

Turn the dough out onto a lightly floured work surface and pat it into a disk. Divide it into thirds. Lightly moisten your hands with water and gently roll one portion of dough into a rough oval. Place it crosswise on the baking sheet and use your hands and fingers to stretch and pat the dough into a log about

2 in/5 cm wide and 10 in/25 cm long. Shape the remaining pieces of dough in the same way, moistening your hands as necessary. Press down on the logs to flatten them out a bit and make the tops even.

Bake the logs for 25 to 30 minutes, or until they are just set—they should be springy to the touch and there should be cracks on the surface. Transfer the baking sheet to a cooling rack. Gently slide an offset spatula under each log to loosen it from the baking sheet. Let the logs cool for 5 minutes, and then transfer them to the rack and let cool for 20 minutes. Lower the oven temperature to 300°F/150°C.

Transfer the cooled logs to a cutting board and, using a Santoku knife or a serrated bread knife, cut them on the diagonal into ½-in-/12-mm-thick slices. Arrange the slices, cut-side up, on the baking sheet (in batches if necessary) and bake for 15 minutes. Turn the slices over and bake for another 10 minutes, until they are crisp. Transfer the slices to the rack to cool completely. The biscotti will keep for up to 10 days in an airtight container stored at room temperature.

WHAT TO DRINK: Cynar, a pleasantly bitter Italian liqueur made from artichokes.

★

2 LARGE EGGS, LIGHTLY BEATEN

2 TSP PURE ALMOND EXTRACT

4 OZ/115 G BITTERSWEET CHOCOLATE, MELTED (SEE PAGE 17) AND COOLED SLIGHTLY

MAKES ABOUT **42** BISCOTTI

CHOCOLATE CHUNK

WITH CHERRIES

★

1 TBSP VEGETABLE OIL

2 CUPS/255 G
UNBLEACHED
ALL-PURPOSE FLOUR

¾ CUP/150 G SUGAR

1 TSP BAKING POWDER

¼ TSP FINE SEA SALT

¾ CUP/105 G HAZELNUTS
OR WHOLE ALMONDS, OR A
MIX OF THE TWO, TOASTED
(SEE PAGE 16)

¾ CUP/95 G DRIED TART
CHERRIES

6 TBSP/85 G UNSALTED
BUTTER, CUT INTO
½-IN/12-MM PIECES, AT
COOL ROOM TEMPERATURE

2 LARGE EGGS,
LIGHTLY BEATEN

If you have ever enjoyed chocolate-covered dried cherries—my family eats more than our fair share every summer in Michigan, where tart cherries are abundant—you will love these rich, chewy biscotti. They are at their fudgiest when baked once, but you can bake them twice to bring out the toasty flavor of the nuts.

Heat the oven to 350°F/180°C. Lightly coat an 11-by-17-in/ 28-by-43-cm rimmed baking sheet with the oil.

Combine the flour, sugar, baking powder, and salt in the bowl of a stand mixer fitted with the paddle attachment. Mix briefly on low speed. Add the hazelnuts and dried cherries and mix briefly on low to combine. Add the butter in pieces and mix until incorporated. Pour in the eggs and mix on medium-low speed until the mixture begins to come together. Add the melted chocolate and chocolate chunks and mix on medium-low speed until a soft, slightly sticky dough has formed.

Turn the dough out onto a lightly floured work surface and pat it into a disk. Divide it in half. Lightly moisten your hands with water and gently roll one portion of dough into a rough oval. Place it lengthwise on the baking sheet and use your hands and fingers to stretch and pat the dough into a log about 2½ in/6 cm wide and 11 to 12 in/28 to 30 cm long. Shape the second piece of dough in the same way, moistening your hands as necessary. Press down on the logs to flatten them out a bit and make the tops even.

CONT'D

4 OZ/115 G BITTERSWEET
CHOCOLATE, MELTED
(SEE PAGE 17) AND
COOLED SLIGHTLY

2 OZ/55 G SEMISWEET OR
BITTERSWEET CHOCOLATE,
CUT INTO SMALL CHUNKS

MAKES ABOUT **40** BISCOTTI

Bake the logs for 25 minutes, or until they are just set—they should be springy to the touch and there should be cracks on the surface. Transfer the baking sheet to a cooling rack. Gently slide an offset spatula under each log to loosen it from the baking sheet. Let the logs cool for 5 minutes, and then transfer them to the rack and let cool for 20 minutes. If baking the logs twice, lower the oven temperature to 325°F/165°C.

Transfer the cooled logs to a cutting board and, using a Santoku knife or a serrated bread knife, cut them on the diagonal into ½-in-/12-mm-thick slices. If you wish, arrange the slices, cut-side up, on the baking sheet (in batches if necessary) and bake for 10 minutes. Turn the slices over and bake for another 10 minutes, until they are crisp. Transfer the slices to the rack to cool completely. If baked once, the biscotti will keep for up 3 days in an airtight container stored at room temperature; if baked twice, they will keep for up to 10 days.

WHAT TO DRINK: Cold milk or hot chocolate.

LEMON

AND

CHOCOLATE

Though it might seem an odd pairing, chocolate and lemon appear together often in Italian cookies, and with good reason. They make a winning combination. It takes a bit of practice to master twisting the sticky ropes of dough together to create the two-tone effect, but it's not difficult. And the resulting cookies are as pretty as they are tasty.

Heat the oven to 350°F/180°C. Lightly coat an 11-by-17-in/28-by-43-cm rimmed baking sheet with the oil.

Combine the flour, sugar, baking powder, and salt in the bowl of a stand mixer fitted with the paddle attachment. Add the almonds and mix on low speed to combine. Add the butter in pieces and mix on medium-low speed until the mixture looks like damp sand. Add the eggs and vanilla and mix on medium speed until a soft, slightly sticky dough has formed. Scoop out half the dough and set it aside in a separate bowl.

Add the lemon zest and lemon extract to the dough remaining in the mixer and mix on medium-low speed until combined. Scoop the lemon dough from the mixing bowl, set it on a lightly floured work surface, and pat it into a disk. Return the other piece of dough to the mixing bowl. Add the cocoa powder and melted chocolate and mix on medium-low speed until fully incorporated. Scoop the chocolate dough onto the work surface and pat it into a disk. Cut each disk in half so that you have four pieces of dough. Using lightly floured hands, roll,

1 TBSP VEGETABLE OIL

2 CUPS/255 G
UNBLEACHED
ALL-PURPOSE FLOUR

1 CUP/200 G SUGAR

1 TSP BAKING POWDER

¼ TSP FINE SEA SALT

1 CUP/140 G WHOLE
ALMONDS, TOASTED
(SEE PAGE 16)

2 TBSP UNSALTED BUTTER,
CUT INTO ½-IN/12-MM
PIECES, AT COOL ROOM
TEMPERATURE

2 LARGE EGGS,
LIGHTLY BEATEN

½ TSP PURE VANILLA
EXTRACT

CONT'D

FINELY GRATED ZEST OF
1 ORGANIC LEMON

½ TSP PURE LEMON
EXTRACT

2 TBSP UNSWEETENED
COCOA POWDER

2 OZ/85 G BITTERSWEET
CHOCOLATE, MELTED
(SEE PAGE 17) AND
COOLED SLIGHTLY

MAKES ABOUT 40 BISCOTTI

pat, and stretch each piece into a thin rope about 14 in/35 cm long and 1 in/2 cm wide.

Bring together one chocolate and one lemon rope and carefully twist them together several times. If the ropes break at any point, just pat them back together. Pat the twisted ropes together until you have a uniform log about 2 in/5 cm wide and 14 in/35 cm long. Set the log on one side of the baking sheet. Make a second log with the remaining two ropes in the same way and set it on the other side of the baking sheet. Press down on the logs to flatten them out a bit and make the tops even.

Bake the logs for 25 minutes, or until they are just set—they should be springy to the touch and there should be cracks on the surface. Transfer the baking sheet to a cooling rack. Gently slide an offset spatula under each log to loosen it from the baking sheet. Let the logs cool for 5 minutes, and then transfer them to the rack and let cool for 20 minutes. Lower the oven temperature to 300°F/150°C.

Transfer the cooled logs to a cutting board and, using a Santoku knife or a serrated bread knife, cut them on the diagonal into ½-in-/12-mm-thick slices. Arrange the slices, cut-side up, on the baking sheet (in batches if necessary) and bake for 15 minutes. Turn the slices over and bake for another 15 minutes, until they are crisp. Transfer the slices to the rack to cool completely. The biscotti will keep for up to 10 days in an airtight container stored at room temperature.

WHAT TO DRINK: Limoncello or a shot of espresso garnished with a strip of lemon zest.

CHOCOLATE- GINGER

★

1 TBSP VEGETABLE OIL

2 CUPS/255 G
UNBLEACHED
ALL-PURPOSE FLOUR

¾ CUP/150 G
LIGHTLY PACKED LIGHT
BROWN SUGAR

2 TSP GROUND GINGER

1 TSP BAKING POWDER

¼ TSP FINE SEA SALT

1 CUP/115 G SLICED
HONEY-ROASTED ALMONDS

½ CUP/85 G FINELY
CHOPPED CRYSTALLIZED
GINGER

6 TBSP/85 G UNSALTED
BUTTER, CUT INTO
½-IN/12-MM PIECES, AT
COOL ROOM TEMPERATURE

My dad and I are both lovers of ginger, especially around Christmastime, when we insist on something gingery on the cookie plate. These crispy biscotti get a triple blast of our favorite spice—ground, fresh, and crystallized. The chocolate is less pronounced, but it rounds out the flavors nicely. You can find honey-roasted almonds at Trader Joe's and other markets.

Heat the oven to 350°F/180°C. Lightly coat an 11-by-17-in/ 28-by-43-cm rimmed baking sheet with the oil.

Combine the flour, brown sugar, ground ginger, baking powder, and salt in the bowl of a stand mixer fitted with the paddle attachment. Mix briefly on low speed. Add the almonds and crystallized ginger and mix briefly on low to combine. Add the butter in pieces and mix until incorporated. Pour in the eggs, melted chocolate, and grated ginger and mix on medium speed until a soft, sticky dough has formed.

Turn the dough out onto a lightly floured work surface and pat it into a disk. Divide it in half. Lightly moisten your hands with water and gently roll one portion into a rough oval. Place it lengthwise on one half of the baking sheet and use your hands and fingers to stretch and pat the dough into a log about 2½ in/6 cm wide and 12 in/30 cm long. Shape the second piece of dough in the same way, moistening your hands as necessary. Press down on the logs to flatten them out a bit and make the tops even.

Bake the logs for 25 minutes, or until they are just set—they should be springy to the touch and there should be cracks on the surface. Transfer the baking sheet to a cooling rack. Gently slide an offset spatula under each log to loosen it from the baking sheet. Let the logs cool for 5 minutes, and then transfer them to the rack and let cool for 20 minutes. Lower the oven temperature to 300°F/150°C.

Transfer the cooled logs to a cutting board and, using a Santoku knife or a serrated bread knife, cut them on the diagonal into ½-in-/12-mm-thick slices. Arrange the slices, cut-side up, on the baking sheet (in batches if necessary) and bake for 15 minutes. Turn the slices over and bake for another 10 minutes, until they are crisp. Transfer the slices to the rack to cool completely. The biscotti will keep for up to 10 days in an airtight container stored at room temperature.

WHAT TO DRINK: If you can find it, try Punch Abruzzo, a citrus-and-caramel-infused liqueur from Italy's Abruzzo region; otherwise, Grand Marnier or even a cup of strong American coffee would be good.

★

2 LARGE EGGS, LIGHTLY BEATEN

4 OZ/115 G BITTERSWEET CHOCOLATE, MELTED (SEE PAGE 17) AND COOLED SLIGHTLY

1 TBSP GRATED FRESH GINGER

MAKES ABOUT BISCOTTI

CHOCOLATE-STUDDED

1 TBSP VEGETABLE OIL

2 CUPS/255 G UNBLEACHED ALL-PURPOSE FLOUR

¾ CUP/150 G SUGAR

1 TSP BAKING POWDER

¼ TSP FINE SEA SALT

5 TBSP/70 G UNSALTED BUTTER, CUT INTO ½-IN/12-MM PIECES, AT COOL ROOM TEMPERATURE

3 LARGE EGGS, LIGHTLY BEATEN

½ TSP PURE ALMOND EXTRACT

½ TSP PURE VANILLA EXTRACT

4 OZ/115 G BITTERSWEET CHOCOLATE, CUT INTO SMALL CHUNKS

MAKES ABOUT 48 BISCOTTI

Instead of nuts, these two-bite biscotti are studded with pieces of bittersweet chocolate. This recipe started out as a favor to my son, who doesn't love nuts in baked goods. I was skeptical—after all, nuts, especially almonds, are considered a central ingredient in biscotti. Turns out, though, the kid was right. These biscotti make great dunkers.

Heat the oven to 350°F/180°C. Lightly coat an 11-by-17-in/28-by-43-cm rimmed baking sheet with the oil.

Combine the flour, sugar, baking powder, and salt in the bowl of a stand mixer fitted with the paddle attachment. Mix briefly on low speed. Add the butter in pieces and mix on medium-low speed until the mixture looks like damp sand. Set aside 1 Tbsp of the beaten eggs. Pour the remaining eggs, the almond extract, and vanilla into the mixing bowl and mix on medium speed until a soft, slightly sticky dough has formed. Add the chocolate chunks and mix on low speed just until incorporated.

Turn the dough out onto a lightly floured work surface and pat it into a disk. Divide it into quarters. Lightly moisten your hands with water and gently roll one portion of dough into a rough oval. Place it crosswise on the baking sheet and use your hands and fingers to stretch and pat the dough into a log about 1½ in/4 cm wide and 9 in/23 cm long. Shape the remaining pieces of dough in the same way, moistening your hands as necessary. Set the logs crosswise on the baking sheet, leaving at least 2 in/5 cm between them. Press down on the logs to flatten them out a bit and make the tops even. Lightly brush the tops of the logs with the reserved beaten egg.

CONT'D

CON GOCCIE DI CIOCCOLATO

Bake the logs for 20 minutes, or until they are lightly browned and just set—they should be springy to the touch and there should be cracks on the surface. Transfer the baking sheet to a cooling rack. Gently slide an offset spatula under each log to loosen it from the baking sheet. Let the logs cool for 5 minutes, and then transfer them to the racks and let cool for 20 minutes. Lower the oven temperature to 300°F/150°C.

Transfer the cooled logs to a cutting board and, using a Santoku knife or a serrated bread knife, cut them on the diagonal into ¾-in-/2-cm-thick slices. Arrange the slices, cut-side up, on the baking sheet (in batches if necessary) and bake for 10 minutes. Turn the slices over and bake for another 9 to 10 minutes, until they are crisp. Transfer the slices to the rack to cool completely. The biscotti will keep for up to 10 days in an airtight container stored at room temperature.

WHAT TO DRINK: Vin Santo, espresso, or a glass of cold milk.

BROWNED BUTTER AND
TOBLERONE

My friend Laura has a wonderful baking blog called Tutti Dolci, which means "all sweets" in Italian. One day, while reading the blog's archives, I came across a recipe for biscotti with chopped Toblerone chocolate folded into the dough. Brilliant! Laura generously gave me the go-ahead to share the recipe here.

Combine the flour, baking powder, and salt in a medium bowl and whisk until well incorporated. Set aside.

In a small, heavy-bottomed saucepan, melt the butter over medium-low heat. Continue to cook the butter, stirring continuously, until it foams, turns clear, and then turns a deep brown, 5 to 6 minutes. Remove from the heat immediately and pour it into the bowl of a stand mixer fitted with the paddle attachment. Let the butter cool for 5 to 10 minutes, until it is no longer hot.

Pour the sugar, brandy, vanilla, and almond extract into the bowl and beat on low speed until combined. Add the eggs, one at a time, and beat until combined. Dump in the flour mixture and beat on low speed until a soft, sticky dough has formed (it will be very soft). Toss in the chopped Toblerone bar and mix on low just until incorporated. Using a spatula, scrape the dough onto a sheet of wax paper or plastic wrap. Pat it into a disk, wrap, and set in the refrigerator to chill for 30 to 60 minutes.

Heat the oven to 350°F/180°C. Lightly coat an 11-by-17-in/ 28-by-43-cm baking sheet with the oil.

CONT'D

★

2¾ CUPS/340 G UNBLEACHED ALL-PURPOSE FLOUR

1½ TSP BAKING POWDER

½ TSP FINE SEA SALT

8 TBSP/115 G UNSALTED BUTTER

¾ CUP/150 G SUGAR

1 TBSP BRANDY

2 TSP PURE VANILLA EXTRACT

1 TSP PURE ALMOND EXTRACT

3 LARGE EGGS

ONE 3.52-OZ/100-G TOBLERONE BAR, CUT INTO SMALL PIECES

1 TBSP VEGETABLE OIL

4 OZ/115 G SEMISWEET
CHOCOLATE, MELTED
(SEE PAGE 17)

MAKES ABOUT
32
LARGE BISCOTTI

Cut the chilled dough in half. Place one portion on one half of the baking sheet and use your hands and fingers to roll, stretch, and pat the dough into a log about 4 in/10 cm wide and 10 in/25 cm long. Shape the second piece of dough in the same way. Press down on the logs to flatten them out a bit and make the tops even.

Bake the logs for 25 minutes, or until they are just set—they should be springy to the touch and there should be cracks on the surface. Transfer the baking sheet to a cooling rack. Gently slide an offset spatula under each log to loosen it from the baking sheet. Let the logs cool for 5 minutes, and then transfer them to the rack and let cool for 20 minutes. Lower the oven temperature to 325°F/165°C.

Transfer the cooled logs to a cutting board and, using a Santoku knife or a serrated bread knife, cut them on the diagonal into ½-in-/12-mm-thick slices. Arrange the slices, cut-side up, on the baking sheet (in batches if necessary) and bake for 8 minutes. Turn the slices over and bake for another 8 minutes, until they are crisp and golden brown. Transfer the slices to the rack to cool completely.

Arrange the slices cut-side up on a baking sheet lined with wax paper. Dip a fork into the melted chocolate and wave it back and forth over the biscotti to create drizzles and droplets (you may not use all the melted chocolate, depending on how much drizzle you want). Place the baking sheet in the refrigerator for 30 minutes for the chocolate to set. Let the biscotti return to room temperature before serving. The biscotti will keep for up to 10 days in an airtight container stored at room temperature.

WHAT TO DRINK: Perfect with a shot of espresso on a cold afternoon.

STRACCIATELLA

1 TBSP VEGETABLE OIL

2 CUPS/255 G
UNBLEACHED
ALL-PURPOSE FLOUR

¾ CUP/70 G ALMOND
FLOUR OR ALMOND MEAL
(SEE PAGE 14)

½ CUP/100 G
GRANULATED SUGAR

¼ CUP/55 G FIRMLY
PACKED DARK BROWN
SUGAR

1 TSP BAKING POWDER

¼ TSP SALT

¾ CUP/75 G SLICED
ALMONDS, TOASTED
(SEE PAGE 16)

2 OZ/55 G BITTERSWEET
CHOCOLATE, SHAVED
USING THE LARGE HOLES
OF A BOX GRATER, PLUS
4 OZ/110 G, MELTED
(SEE PAGE 17; OPTIONAL)

You might be familiar with stracciatella gelato—vanilla ice cream shot through with chocolate shavings. This is something similar but in the form of biscotti, with chocolate shavings mixed right into the dough. The dough is enriched with almond flour and extra butter, making these biscotti more tender than most. The bittersweet chocolate drizzle is an optional flourish, but I think it provides a nice contrast to the cookie's richness.

Heat the oven to 350°F/180°C. Lightly coat an 11-by-17-in/ 28-by-43-cm baking sheet with the oil.

Combine the all-purpose flour, almond flour, granulated sugar, brown sugar, baking powder, and salt in the bowl of a stand mixer fitted with the paddle attachment. Mix briefly on low speed. Add the almonds and shaved chocolate and mix briefly on low to combine. Add the butter in pieces and mix on medium-low speed until the mixture looks like damp sand. Pour in the eggs, almond extract, and vanilla and mix on medium speed until a soft, sticky dough has formed (this butter-rich dough is extra-sticky).

Turn the dough out onto a lightly floured work surface and pat it into a disk. Divide it in half. Lightly moisten your hands with water and gently roll one portion of dough into a rough oval. Place it lengthwise on one half of the baking sheet and use your hands and fingers to stretch and pat the dough into a log about 2½ in/6 cm wide and 12 in/30 cm long. Shape the second piece of dough in the same way, moistening your hands as necessary. Press down on the logs to flatten them out a bit and make the tops even.

Bake the logs for 25 minutes, or until they are just set—they should be springy to the touch and there should be cracks on the surface. Transfer the baking sheet to a cooling rack. Gently slide an offset spatula under each log to loosen it from the baking sheet. Let the logs cool for 5 minutes, and then transfer them to the rack and let cool for 20 minutes. Lower the oven temperature to 300°F/150°C.

Transfer the cooled logs to a cutting board and, using a Santoku knife or a serrated bread knife, cut them on the diagonal into ⅜-in-/1-cm-thick slices. Arrange the slices, cut-side up, on the baking sheet (in batches if necessary) and bake for 8 minutes. Turn the slices over and bake for another 8 minutes, until they are crisp and golden brown. Transfer the slices to the rack to cool completely.

If you are drizzling the biscotti with chocolate, arrange the slices cut-side up on a baking sheet lined with wax paper. Dip a fork into the melted chocolate and wave it back and forth over the biscotti to create drizzles and droplets (you may not use all the melted chocolate, depending on how much drizzle you want). Place the baking sheet in the refrigerator for 30 minutes for the chocolate to set. Let the biscotti return to room temperature before serving. The biscotti will keep for up to 10 days in an airtight container stored at room temperature.

WHAT TO DRINK: Freshly brewed coffee or cold milk.

★

8 TBSP/115 G UNSALTED BUTTER, CUT INTO ½-IN/12-MM PIECES, AT COOL ROOM TEMPERATURE

2 LARGE EGGS, LIGHTLY BEATEN

1 TSP PURE ALMOND EXTRACT

¼ TSP PURE VANILLA EXTRACT

MAKES ABOUT 50 BISCOTTI

BISCOTTI WITH FRUIT

ICED TRIPLE
LEMON

1 TBSP VEGETABLE OIL

2¼ CUPS/285 G
UNBLEACHED
ALL-PURPOSE FLOUR

½ CUP/100 G
GRANULATED SUGAR

¼ CUP/50 G FIRMLY
PACKED LIGHT BROWN
SUGAR

1 TSP BAKING POWDER

¼ TSP FINE SEA SALT

FINELY GRATED ZEST
OF 2 ORGANIC LEMONS,
PLUS 3 TBSP FRESHLY
SQUEEZED JUICE

1 CUP/80 G SLICED
ALMONDS, TOASTED
(SEE PAGE 16)

8 TBSP/115 G UNSALTED
BUTTER, AT COOL ROOM
TEMPERATURE, CUT INTO
½-IN/12-MM PIECES

I did not love lemon desserts when I was a child. Chocolate was much more my thing. Not surprisingly, my tastes have changed and now I count lemon tarts, cakes, and cookies among my favorites—especially these biscotti. Crisp and buttery, they are layered with bright flavor from lemon juice, zest, and extract. Once cooled, they get an additional shot of lemon with a drizzle of tangy icing.

Heat the oven to 350°F/180°C. Lightly coat an 11-by-17-in/ 28-by-43-cm rimmed baking sheet with the oil.

Combine the flour, granulated sugar, brown sugar, baking powder, and salt in the bowl of a stand mixer fitted with the paddle attachment. Mix briefly on low speed. Add the lemon zest and almonds and mix briefly on low to combine. Add the butter in pieces and mix on medium-low speed until the mixture looks like damp sand. Pour in the eggs, 1 Tbsp of the lemon juice, and 1 tsp of the lemon extract and mix on medium speed until a soft, slightly sticky dough has formed.

Turn the dough out onto a lightly floured work surface and pat it into a disk. Divide it in half. Lightly moisten your hands with water and gently roll one portion of dough into a rough oval. Place it lengthwise on one half of the baking sheet and use your hands and fingers to stretch and pat the dough into a log about 2½ in/6 cm wide and 12 in/30 cm long. Shape the second piece of dough in the same way, moistening your hands as necessary. Press down on the logs to flatten them out a bit and make the tops even.

CONT'D

GLASSATO AL

LIMONE

**2 LARGE EGGS,
LIGHTLY BEATEN**

**1¼ TSP PURE LEMON
EXTRACT**

**1 CUP/100 G
CONFECTIONERS' SUGAR,
SIFTED**

**A FEW DROPS OF
HALF-AND-HALF OR MILK,
AS NEEDED**

MAKES 24 TO 26 BISCOTTI

Bake the logs for 25 minutes, or until they are lightly browned and just set—they should be springy to the touch and there should be cracks on the surface. Transfer the baking sheet to a cooling rack. Gently slide an offset spatula under each log to loosen it from the baking sheet. Let the logs cool for 5 minutes, and then transfer them to the rack and let cool for 20 minutes. Lower the oven temperature to 325°F/165°C.

Transfer the cooled logs to a cutting board and, using a Santoku knife or a serrated bread knife, cut them on the diagonal into ¾-in-/2-cm-thick slices. Arrange the slices, cut-side up, on the baking sheet (in batches if necessary) and bake for 10 minutes. Turn the slices over and bake for another 10 minutes, until they are crisp. Transfer the slices to the rack to cool completely.

Place the rack over a rimmed baking sheet or a sheet of wax paper. Arrange the slices upright on the rack. In a small bowl, whisk together the confectioners' sugar with the remaining 2 Tbsp lemon juice and ¼ tsp lemon extract until the icing is smooth and opaque, but still thin enough to fall from the tip of the whisk in a ribbon. If necessary, dribble in a few drops of half-and-half to loosen the icing.

Dip the tip of the whisk or a fork into the icing and drizzle the ribbon of icing back and forth over the biscotti. Let the icing dry completely before serving. The biscotti will keep for up to 10 days in an airtight container stored at room temperature.

WHAT TO DRINK: A small glass of Strega, a saffron-tinged herbal liqueur from Italy's Campania region; or, for something more conventional, a glass of limoncello.

COCONUT-LIME

Unconventional? Totally. And yet, I'm pretty sure these crisp, delicately flavored biscotti would be at home on an Italian dessert table. After all, coconut gelato is a favorite flavor in Italy, so why not biscotti?

Heat the oven to 350°F/180°C. Lightly coat an 11-by-17-in/ 28-by-43-cm rimmed baking sheet with the oil.

    Combine the flour, sugar, coconut, baking powder, and salt in the bowl of a stand mixer fitted with the paddle attachment. Mix briefly on low speed. Add the almonds and lime zest and mix briefly on low to combine. Add the butter in pieces and mix on medium-low speed until the mixture looks like damp sand. Pour in the eggs and lime juice and mix on medium speed until a soft, slightly sticky dough has formed.

    Turn the dough out onto a lightly floured work surface and pat it into a disk. Divide it into quarters. Lightly moisten your hands with water and gently roll one portion of dough into a rough oval. Place it crosswise on one half of the baking sheet and use your hands and fingers to stretch and pat the dough into a log about 1½ in/4 cm wide and 9 in/23 cm long. Shape the remaining pieces of dough in the same way, moistening your hands as necessary. Press down on the logs to flatten them out a bit and make the tops even.

CONT'D

★

1 TBSP VEGETABLE OIL

2½ CUPS/315 G UNBLEACHED ALL-PURPOSE FLOUR

¾ CUP/150 G SUGAR

½ CUP/55 G SHREDDED UNSWEETENED COCONUT

1 TSP BAKING POWDER

¼ TSP FINE SEA SALT

¾ CUP/75 G SLICED ALMONDS, TOASTED (SEE PAGE 16)

FINELY GRATED ZEST OF 2 ORGANIC LIMES, PLUS THE JUICE OF 1 LIME

COCCO E LIME

Bake the logs for 15 minutes, or until the bottom edges are lightly browned and the tops are set—they should be springy to the touch and there should be cracks on the surface. Transfer the baking sheet to a cooling rack. Gently slide an offset spatula under each log to loosen it from the baking sheet. Let the logs cool for 5 minutes, and then transfer them to the rack and let cool for 20 minutes. Lower the oven temperature to 300°F/150°C.

Transfer the cooled logs to a cutting board and, using a Santoku knife or a serrated bread knife, cut them on the diagonal into ⅜-in-/1-cm-thick slices. Arrange the slices, cut-side up, on the baking sheet (in batches if necessary) and bake for 8 minutes. Turn the slices over and bake for another 8 minutes, until they are crisp. Transfer the slices to the rack to cool completely. The biscotti will keep for up to 10 days in an airtight container stored at room temperature.

WHAT TO DRINK: Cardamaro, a pleasantly bitter wine-based *digestivo* made with cardoons.

★

6 TBSP/85 G UNSALTED BUTTER, CUT INTO ½-IN/12-MM PIECES, AT COOL ROOM TEMPERATURE

2 LARGE EGGS, LIGHTLY BEATEN

MAKES
70 TO 80
SMALL BISCOTTI

CHOCOLATE-DIPPED
TOASTED COCONUT

★

1 TBSP VEGETABLE OIL

2¼ CUPS/285 G
UNBLEACHED
ALL-PURPOSE FLOUR

¾ CUP/50 G
UNSWEETENED COCONUT
FLAKES, TOASTED
(SEE PAGE 16)

¾ CUP/150 G SUGAR

1 TSP BAKING POWDER

¼ TSP FINE SEA SALT

½ CUP/50 G SLICED
HONEY-ROASTED ALMONDS
OR SLICED ALMONDS,
TOASTED (SEE PAGE 16)

I created these biscotti for my sister, Maria, lover of all things coconut. Big flakes of coconut, toasted in the oven, give these cookies a rich aroma and extra crunch. If you like, you can enjoy them plain, without the bittersweet chocolate dip. The honey-roasted almonds can be found at Trader Joe's and other markets.

Heat the oven to 350°F/180°C. Lightly coat an 11-by-17-in/28-by-43-cm rimmed baking sheet with the oil.

Combine the flour, coconut, sugar, baking powder, and salt in the bowl of a stand mixer fitted with the paddle attachment. Mix briefly on low speed. Add the almonds and mix briefly on low to combine. Add the butter in pieces and mix on medium-low speed until the mixture looks like damp sand. Pour in the eggs and mix on medium speed until a soft, slightly sticky dough has formed.

Turn the dough out onto a lightly floured work surface and pat it into a disk. Divide it in half. Lightly moisten your hands with water and gently roll one portion of dough into a rough oval. Place it lengthwise on one half of the baking sheet and use your hands and fingers to stretch and pat the dough into a log about 2½ in/6 cm wide and 12 in/30 cm long. Shape the second piece of dough in the same way, moistening your hands as necessary. Press down on the logs to flatten them out a bit and make the tops even.

CONT'D

5 TBSP/70 G UNSALTED
BUTTER CUT INTO
½-IN/12-MM PIECES, AT
COOL ROOM TEMPERATURE

2 LARGE EGGS,
LIGHTLY BEATEN

4 OZ/115 G BITTERSWEET
CHOCOLATE, MELTED
(SEE PAGE 17; OPTIONAL)

MAKES **36** TO **40** BISCOTTI

Bake the logs for 25 minutes, or until the bottom edges are lightly browned and the tops are set—they should be springy to the touch and there should be cracks on the surface. Transfer the baking sheet to a cooling rack. Gently slide an offset spatula under each log to loosen it from the baking sheet. Let the logs cool for 5 minutes, and then transfer them to the rack and let cool for 20 minutes. Lower the oven temperature to 300°F/150°C.

Transfer the cooled logs to a cutting board and, using a Santoku knife or a serrated bread knife, cut them on the diagonal into ½-in-/12-mm-thick slices. Arrange the slices, cut-side up, on the baking sheet (in batches if necessary) and bake for 10 minutes. Turn the slices over and bake for another 10 to 15 minutes, until they are crisp and golden. Transfer the slices to the rack to cool completely.

Arrange the slices cut-side up on a baking sheet lined with wax paper. Dip one end of each biscotto into the melted chocolate and set them on the wax paper. Place the baking sheet in the refrigerator for 30 minutes, or until the chocolate is set. Let the biscotti return to room temperature before serving. The biscotti will keep for up to 10 days in an airtight container stored at room temperature.

WHAT TO DRINK: Baileys Irish Cream—don't knock it, it works.

CHRISTMAS
CRANBERRY-PISTACHIO

Ever since biscotti invaded American cookie trays a couple of decades ago, this holiday combination of pistachios, tart cranberries, and orange zest has become a classic. A drizzle of orange-spiked glaze makes them even more festive.

Heat the oven to 350°F/180°C. Lightly coat an 11-by-17-in/ 28-by-43-cm rimmed baking sheet with the oil.

Combine the flour, granulated sugar, baking powder, cinnamon, and salt in the bowl of a stand mixer fitted with the paddle attachment. Mix briefly on low speed. Set aside ¼ tsp of the orange zest. Add the remaining zest, the pistachios, and cranberries and mix briefly on low to combine. Add the butter in pieces and mix on medium-low speed until the mixture looks like damp sand. Pour in the eggs and 1 Tbsp of the orange juice and mix on medium speed until a soft, slightly sticky dough has formed.

Turn the dough out onto a lightly floured work surface and pat it into a disk. Divide it in half. Lightly moisten your hands with water and gently roll one portion of dough into a rough oval. Place it lengthwise on one half of the baking sheet and use your hands and fingers to stretch and pat the dough into a log about 2½ in/6 cm wide and 12 in/30 cm long. Shape the second piece of dough in the same way, moistening your hands as necessary. Press down on the logs to flatten them out a bit and make the tops even.

CONT'D

★

1 TBSP VEGETABLE OIL

2¼ CUPS/285 G UNBLEACHED ALL-PURPOSE FLOUR

¾ CUP/150 G GRANULATED SUGAR

1 TSP BAKING POWDER

½ TSP GROUND CINNAMON

¼ TSP FINE SEA SALT

FINELY GRATED ZEST OF 1 ORGANIC ORANGE, PLUS 3 TBSP FRESHLY SQUEEZED JUICE

½ CUP/60 G SHELLED PISTACHIOS

½ CUP/55 G DRIED CRANBERRIES

- 77 -
BISCOTTI WITH FRUIT

8 TBSP/115 G UNSALTED
BUTTER, CUT INTO
½-IN/12-MM PIECES, AT
COOL ROOM TEMPERATURE

2 LARGE EGGS,
LIGHTLY BEATEN

1 CUP/100 G
CONFECTIONERS' SUGAR,
SIFTED

A FEW DROPS OF
HALF-AND-HALF OR MILK,
AS NEEDED

MAKES ABOUT 40 BISCOTTI

Bake the logs for 25 minutes, or until they are lightly browned and just set—they should be springy to the touch and there should be cracks on the surface. Transfer the baking sheet to a cooling rack. Gently slide an offset spatula under each log to loosen it from the baking sheet. Let the logs cool for 5 minutes, and then transfer them to the rack and let cool for 20 minutes. Lower the oven temperature to 300°F/150°C.

Transfer the cooled logs to a cutting board and, using a Santoku knife or a serrated bread knife, cut them on the diagonal into ½-in-/12-mm-thick slices. Arrange the slices, cut-side up, on the baking sheet (in batches if necessary) and bake for 10 minutes. Turn the slices over and bake for another 10 minutes, until they are crisp. Transfer the slices to the rack to cool completely.

Place the rack over a rimmed baking sheet or a sheet of wax paper. Arrange the slices cut-side down on the rack. In a small bowl, whisk together the confectioners' sugar with the remaining 2 Tbsp orange juice and the reserved ¼ tsp orange zest until the icing is smooth and opaque, but still loose enough to fall from the tip of the whisk in a ribbon. If necessary, dribble in a few drops of half-and-half to loosen the icing.

Dip the tip of the whisk or a fork into the icing and drizzle a ribbon of icing back and forth over the biscotti. Let the icing dry completely before serving. The biscotti will keep for up to 10 days in an airtight container stored at room temperature.

WHAT TO DRINK: Eggnog, either homemade or a good-quality brand from a local dairy, if you can find it.

HONEY-ANISE WITH
APRICOTS

★

1 TBSP VEGETABLE OIL

2 CUPS/255 G
UNBLEACHED
ALL-PURPOSE FLOUR

½ CUP/100 G
FIRMLY PACKED LIGHT
BROWN SUGAR

½ TSP BAKING POWDER

⅛ TSP FINE SEA SALT

¾ CUP/95 G CHOPPED
DRIED APRICOTS

½ CUP/70 G WHOLE
ALMONDS, PLUS ½ CUP/
50 G SLICED ALMONDS

FINELY GRATED ZEST OF
1 ORGANIC ORANGE

2 TSP ANISEED

A couple of summers ago I made homemade apricot jam to which I added aniseed. The spice infused the tart jam with a sweet licorice note, and I liked the combination so much that I decided to reprise it here in these biscotti.

Heat the oven to 350°F/180°C. Lightly coat an 11-by-17-in/ 28-by-43-cm rimmed baking sheet with the oil.

Combine the flour, brown sugar, baking powder, and salt in the bowl of a stand mixer fitted with the paddle attachment. Mix briefly on low speed. Add the dried apricots, whole and sliced almonds, orange zest, and aniseed and mix briefly on low to combine. Add the butter in pieces and mix on medium-low speed until the mixture looks like damp sand.

Set aside 1 Tbsp of the beaten eggs. In a small bowl, whisk the honey into the remaining eggs. Add the egg mixture to the flour mixture and mix on medium speed until a soft, slightly sticky dough has formed.

Turn the dough out onto a lightly floured work surface and pat it into a disk. Divide it in half. Lightly moisten your hands with water and gently roll one portion of dough into a rough oval. Place it lengthwise on one half of the baking sheet and use your hands and fingers to stretch and pat the dough into a log about 2½ in/6 cm wide and 12 in/30 cm long. Shape the second piece of dough in the same way, moistening your hands as necessary. Press down on the logs to flatten them out a bit and make the tops even. Brush the tops lightly with the reserved beaten egg.

Bake the logs for 25 minutes, or until they are lightly browned and just set—they should be springy to the touch and there should be cracks on the surface. Transfer the baking sheet to a cooling rack. Gently slide an offset spatula under each log to loosen it from the baking sheet. Let the logs cool for 5 minutes, and then transfer them to the rack and let cool for 20 minutes. Lower the oven temperature to 300°F/150°C.

Transfer the cooled logs to a cutting board and, using a Santoku knife or a serrated bread knife, cut them on the diagonal into ½-in-/12-mm-thick slices. Arrange the slices, cut-side up, on the baking sheet (in batches if necessary) and bake for 8 to 10 minutes. Turn the slices over and bake for another 8 to 10 minutes, until they are crisp. Transfer the slices to the rack to cool completely. The biscotti will keep for up to 10 days in an airtight container stored at room temperature.

WHAT TO DRINK: A shot of sambuca or a cup of hot tea.

★

4 TBSP/55 G UNSALTED BUTTER, CUT INTO ½-IN/12-MM PIECES, AT COOL ROOM TEMPERATURE

2 LARGE EGGS, LIGHTLY BEATEN

2 TBSP HONEY

MAKES 38 TO 40 BISCOTTI

GOLDEN CORNMEAL WITH
SULTANAS

1 TBSP VEGETABLE OIL

2½ CUPS/315 G
UNBLEACHED
ALL-PURPOSE FLOUR

¾ CUP/150 G SUGAR

2 TBSP FINE CORNMEAL

1 TSP BAKING POWDER

¼ TSP FINE SEA SALT

½ CUP/70 G WHOLE
ALMONDS, TOASTED (SEE
PAGE 16), HALVED
CROSSWISE

½ CUP/85 G PACKED
SULTANAS (GOLDEN RAISINS)

6 TBSP/85 G UNSALTED
BUTTER, CUT INTO
½-IN/12-MM PIECES, AT
COOL ROOM TEMPERATURE

2 LARGE EGGS,
LIGHTLY BEATEN

2 TBSP DRY MARSALA

MAKES ABOUT 50 BISCOTTI

Sultanas are what the British call golden raisins. I like the sound of that word, and I like the small, plump dried fruits, which seem to me to have a more complex flavor than regular raisins. They are especially good when combined with the other two golden ingredients in this recipe—cornmeal and Marsala, a fortified wine from Sicily.

Heat the oven to 350°F/180°C. Lightly coat an 11-by-17-in/ 28-by-43-cm rimmed baking sheet with the oil.

Combine the flour, sugar, cornmeal, baking powder, and salt in the bowl of a stand mixer fitted with the paddle attachment. Mix briefly on low speed. Add the almonds and sultanas and mix briefly on low to combine. Add the butter in pieces and mix on medium-low speed until the mixture looks like damp sand. Pour in the eggs and Marsala and mix on medium speed until a soft, slightly sticky dough has formed.

Turn the dough out onto a lightly floured work surface and pat it into a disk. Divide it in half. Lightly moisten your hands with water and gently roll one portion of dough into a rough oval. Place it lengthwise on one half of the baking sheet and use your hands and fingers to stretch and pat the dough into a log about 3 in/8 cm wide and 12 in/30 cm long. Shape the second piece of dough in the same way, moistening your hands as necessary. Press down on the logs to flatten them out a bit and make the tops even.

Bake the logs for 25 minutes, or until they are lightly browned and just set—they should be springy to the touch and there should be cracks on the surface. Transfer the baking sheet to a cooling rack. Gently slide an offset spatula under each log to loosen it from the baking sheet. Let the logs cool for 5 minutes, and then transfer them to the rack and let cool for 20 minutes. Lower the oven temperature to 325°F/165°C.

Transfer the cooled logs to a cutting board and, using a Santoku knife or a serrated bread knife, cut them on the diagonal into ⅓-in-/8-mm-thick slices. Arrange the slices, cut-side up, on the baking sheet (in batches if necessary) and bake for 10 to 12 minutes. Turn the slices over and bake for another 10 to 12 minutes, until they are crisp. Transfer the slices to the rack to cool completely. The biscotti will keep for up to 10 days in an airtight container stored at room temperature.

WHAT TO DRINK: A glass of sherry or Marsala wine.

FIG

AND

FENNEL

I'm going to invoke the W word here: Wholesome. And let us all agree that this is a good thing. Fragrant with orange zest and the warm scent of fennel, these cookies are a great treat to serve on a chilly winter afternoon.

★

1 TBSP VEGETABLE OIL

1½ CUPS/185 G
UNBLEACHED
ALL-PURPOSE FLOUR

½ CUP/60 G
WHOLE-WHEAT FLOUR

¾ CUP/150 G SUGAR

1 TSP BAKING POWDER

2 TSP TOASTED FENNEL
SEEDS (SEE PAGE 16),
LIGHTLY CRUSHED

¼ TSP GROUND CINNAMON

⅛ TSP FINE SEA SALT

FINELY GRATED ZEST
OF 1 ORGANIC ORANGE,
PLUS 2 TBSP FRESHLY
SQUEEZED JUICE

Heat the oven to 350°F/180°C. Lightly coat an 11-by-17-in/ 28-by-43-cm rimmed baking sheet with the oil.

Combine the all-purpose flour, whole-wheat flour, sugar, baking powder, fennel seeds, cinnamon, salt, and orange zest in the bowl of a stand mixer fitted with the paddle attachment. Mix briefly on low speed. Add the almonds and figs and mix briefly on low to combine. Add the butter in pieces and mix on medium-low speed until the mixture looks like damp sand.

Set aside 1 Tbsp of the beaten eggs. In a small bowl, whisk together the remaining eggs and the orange juice. Add the egg mixture to the flour mixture and mix on medium speed until a soft, slightly sticky dough has formed.

Turn the dough out onto a lightly floured work surface and pat it into a disk. Divide it into thirds. Lightly moisten your hands with water and gently roll one portion of dough into a rough oval. Place it crosswise on the baking sheet and use your hands and fingers to stretch and pat the dough into a log about 2 in/5 cm wide and 10 in/25 cm long. Shape the remaining pieces of dough in the same way, moistening your hands as necessary, leaving at least 2 in/5 cm between the logs. Press down on the logs to flatten them out a bit and make the tops even. Lightly brush the tops with the reserved beaten egg.

Bake the logs for 25 minutes, or until they are lightly browned and just set—they should be springy to the touch and there should be cracks on the surface. Transfer the baking sheet to a cooling rack. Gently slide an offset spatula under each log to loosen it from the baking sheet. Let the logs cool for 5 minutes, and then transfer them to the rack and let cool for 20 minutes. Lower the oven temperature to 325°F/165°C.

Transfer the cooled logs to a cutting board and, using a Santoku knife or a serrated bread knife, cut them on the diagonal into ½-in-/12-mm-thick slices. Arrange the slices, cut-side up, on the baking sheet (in batches if necessary) and bake for 8 to 10 minutes. Turn the slices over and bake for another 8 to 10 minutes, until they are crisp. Transfer the slices to the rack to cool completely. The biscotti will keep for up to 10 days in an airtight container stored at room temperature.

WHAT TO DRINK: A mug of hot Earl Grey tea sweetened with honey.

¾ CUP/105 G WHOLE ALMONDS, TOASTED (SEE PAGE 16), HALVED CROSSWISE

½ CUP/80 G CHOPPED DRIED MISSION OR CALIMYRNA FIGS

6 TBSP/85 G UNSALTED BUTTER, CUT INTO ½-IN/12-MM PIECES, AT COOL ROOM TEMPERATURE.

2 LARGE EGGS, LIGHTLY BEATEN

MAKES ABOUT **50** BISCOTTI

FANTASY
FLAVORS

ABCD

(ALMOND, BARLEY, COCONUT, AND DATE)

3 TBSP VEGETABLE OIL, PREFERABLY SUNFLOWER OIL

1½ CUPS/185 G UNBLEACHED ALL-PURPOSE FLOUR

½ CUP/55 G BARLEY FLOUR

¾ CUP/150 G SUGAR

1 TSP BAKING POWDER

¼ TSP FINE SEA SALT

¾ CUP/105 G WHOLE ALMONDS, TOASTED (SEE PAGE 16)

½ CUP/45 G UNSWEETENED COCONUT FLAKES, TOASTED (SEE PAGE 16)

½ CUP/75 G CHOPPED PITTED DATES

I had no idea what to expect when I dreamed up these biscotti in my kitchen one day. I intended them to be an homage of sorts to the Whole Earth Center health foods store in Princeton, New Jersey, that I used to go to with my dad when I was little. The store sold all sorts of healthful ingredients in bulk, displaying them in large open barrels. I'm happy to say that Whole Earth Center is still around. I think these crunchy biscotti have staying power, too, and so are a fitting tribute.

Heat the oven to 350°F/180°C. Lightly coat an 11-by-17-in/ 28-by-43-cm rimmed baking sheet with 1 Tbsp of the oil.

Combine the all-purpose flour, barley flour, sugar, baking powder, and salt in the bowl of a stand mixer fitted with the paddle attachment. Mix briefly on low speed. Add the almonds, coconut, dates, and orange zest and mix on low to combine. Add the eggs, remaining 2 Tbsp oil, and vanilla and mix on medium speed until a soft, slightly sticky dough has formed.

Turn the dough out onto a lightly floured work surface and pat it into a disk. Divide it in half. Lightly moisten your hands with water and gently roll one portion of dough into a rough oval. Place it lengthwise on one half of the baking sheet and use your hands and fingers to stretch and pat the dough into a log about 2 in/5 cm wide and 14 in/35 cm long. Shape the second piece of dough in the same way, moistening your hands as necessary. Press down on the logs to flatten them out a bit and make the tops even.

Bake the logs for 25 minutes, or until they are browned around the edges and just set—they should be springy to the touch and there should be cracks on the surface. Transfer the baking sheet to a cooling rack. Gently slide an offset spatula under each log to loosen it from the baking sheet. Let the logs cool for 5 minutes, and then transfer them to the rack and let cool for 20 minutes. Lower the oven temperature to 300°F/150°C.

Transfer the cooled logs to a cutting board and, using a Santoku knife or a serrated bread knife, cut them on the diagonal into ½-in-/12-mm-thick slices. Arrange the slices, cut-side up, on the baking sheet (in batches if necessary) and bake for 15 minutes. Turn the slices over and bake for another 10 minutes, until they are crisp and golden brown. Transfer the slices to the rack to cool completely. The biscotti will keep for up to 10 days in an airtight container stored at room temperature.

WHAT TO DRINK: Hot mulled cider or a glass of cold cider—freshly pressed, if you can get it.

FINELY GRATED ZEST OF
1 ORGANIC ORANGE

2 LARGE EGGS,
LIGHTLY BEATEN

½ TSP PURE VANILLA
EXTRACT

MAKES **48** TO **50** BISCOTTI

CAPPUCCINO

DUNKERS

These are my homemade answer to the gargantuan biscotti you find at fancy bakeries. They are delicious drizzled with chocolate (see page 64).

1 TBSP VEGETABLE OIL

3 LARGE EGGS

1 TBSP INSTANT ESPRESSO POWDER

¼ TSP PURE VANILLA EXTRACT

2 CUPS/255 G UNBLEACHED ALL-PURPOSE FLOUR

SCANT 1 CUP/200 G SUGAR

½ TSP BAKING POWDER

¼ TSP FINE SEA SALT

¾ CUP/105 G WHOLE ALMONDS, TOASTED (SEE PAGE 16)

MAKES 18 BISCOTTI

Heat the oven to 350°F/180°C. Lightly coat an 11-by-17-in/ 28-by-43-cm rimmed baking sheet with the oil.

In a bowl, whisk together the eggs, espresso powder, and vanilla. Combine the flour, sugar, baking powder, and salt in the bowl of a stand mixer fitted with the paddle attachment. Add the almonds and mix on low speed to combine. Add the egg mixture and mix on medium speed until a soft, sticky dough has formed.

Gather the dough on the baking sheet. Lightly moisten your hands with water and use your fingers to pat the dough into a log about 4½ in/11 cm wide and 12 in/30 cm long.

Bake the log for 20 to 25 minutes, or until lightly browned and just set—it should be springy to the touch and there should be cracks on the surface. Transfer the baking sheet to a cooling rack. Gently slide an offset spatula under the log to loosen it from the baking sheet. Let the log cool for 5 minutes, and then transfer it to the rack and let cool for 20 minutes. Lower the oven temperature to 300°F/150°C.

Transfer the cooled log to a cutting board and, using a Santoku knife or a serrated bread knife, cut it on the diagonal into ¾-in-/2-cm-thick slices. Arrange the slices, cut-side up, on the baking sheet and bake for 15 minutes. Turn the slices over and bake for another 10 to 15 minutes, until they are crisp. Transfer the slices to the rack to cool completely. The biscotti will keep for up to 2 weeks in an airtight container stored at room temperature.

WHAT TO DRINK: Cappuccino, of course!

CARDAMOM-PECAN

★

1 TBSP VEGETABLE OIL

1 CUP/110 G PECAN
HALVES, TOASTED
(SEE PAGE 16)

¾ CUP/150 G SUGAR

2 CUPS/255 G
UNBLEACHED
ALL-PURPOSE FLOUR

1 TSP GROUND CARDAMOM

1 TSP BAKING POWDER

¼ TSP FINE SEA SALT

FINELY GRATED ZEST OF
1 ORGANIC ORANGE

6 TBSP/85 G UNSALTED
BUTTER, CUT INTO
½-IN/12-MM PIECES, AT
COOL ROOM TEMPERATURE

2 LARGE EGGS,
LIGHTLY BEATEN

MAKES ABOUT **42** BISCOTTI

Cardamom is not a spice you expect to find in an Italian cookie. But I am fond of its warm aroma, and I especially like it together with the taste of the pecans in these simple but rich biscotti.

Heat the oven to 350°F/180°C. Lightly coat an 11-by-17-in/28-by-43-cm rimmed baking sheet with the oil.

Combine ½ cup/55 g of the pecans and the sugar in the work bowl of a food processor fitted with the metal blade. Process until the pecans are very finely ground but not so fine that they begin to turn into a paste. Transfer the pulverized pecans and sugar to the bowl of a stand mixer fitted with the paddle attachment. Add the flour, cardamom, baking powder, salt, and orange zest and mix briefly on low speed to combine. Add the remaining ½ cup/55 g pecan halves and mix briefly on low to break up some of the nuts. Add the butter in pieces and mix on medium-low speed until the mixture looks like damp sand. Add the eggs and mix on medium speed until a soft, slightly sticky dough has formed.

Turn the dough out onto a lightly floured work surface and pat it into a disk. Divide it into thirds. Lightly moisten your hands with water and gently roll one portion of dough into a rough oval. Place it crosswise on the baking sheet and use your hands and fingers to stretch and pat the dough into a log about 2 in/5 cm wide and 10 in/25 cm long. Shape the remaining pieces of dough in the same way, moistening your hands as necessary, leaving at least 2 in/5 cm between the logs. Press down on the logs to flatten them out a bit and make the tops even.

Bake the logs for 25 to 30 minutes, or until they are just set—they should be springy to the touch and there should be cracks on the surface. Transfer the baking sheet to a cooling rack. Gently slide an offset spatula under each log to loosen it from the baking sheet. Let the logs cool for 5 minutes, and then transfer them to the rack and let cool for 20 minutes. Lower the oven temperature to 300°F/150°C.

Transfer the cooled logs to a cutting board and, using a Santoku knife or a serrated bread knife, cut them on the diagonal into ½-in-/12-mm-thick slices. Arrange the slices, cut-side up, on the baking sheet (in batches if necessary) and bake for 15 minutes. Turn the slices over and bake for another 10 minutes, until they are crisp. Transfer the slices to the rack to cool completely. The biscotti will keep for up to 10 days in an airtight container stored at room temperature.

WHAT TO DRINK: A cup of chai.

GREEN TEA

WITH WHITE CHOCOLATE GLAZE

★

1 TBSP VEGETABLE OIL

2 TO 2¼ CUPS/
255 TO 285 G
UNBLEACHED
ALL-PURPOSE FLOUR

¾ CUP/150 G
GRANULATED SUGAR

2 TBSP SWEET MATCHA
POWDER

1 TSP BAKING POWDER

¼ TSP FINE SEA SALT

¾ CUP/105 G BLANCHED
(PEELED) WHOLE ALMONDS,
TOASTED (SEE PAGE 16),
HALVED CROSSWISE

4 TBSP/55 G UNSALTED
BUTTER, CUT INTO
½-IN/12-MM PIECES, AT
COOL ROOM TEMPERATURE

2 LARGE EGGS,
LIGHTLY BEATEN

½ TSP PURE VANILLA
EXTRACT

Matcha—Japanese green tea powder—has acquired new life as a dessert ingredient, mixed into cakes, frosting, and even gelato. It also makes great biscotti. Incorporated into basic biscotti dough, the ground green tea imparts a sweet, earthy undertone and, as a bonus, an appealing pale green hue. This recipe uses matcha powder that comes already sweetened with sugar; you can find it at many Asian supermarkets, as well as some well-stocked supermarkets, tea and spice shops, and online.

Heat the oven to 350°F/180°C. Lightly coat an 11-by-17-in/28-by-43-cm rimmed baking sheet with the oil.

Combine 2 cups/255 g of the flour, the granulated sugar, sweet matcha powder, baking powder, and salt in the bowl of a stand mixer fitted with the paddle attachment. Mix briefly on low speed. Add the almonds and mix briefly on low to combine. Add the butter in pieces and mix on medium-low speed until the mixture looks like damp sand. Add the eggs and vanilla and mix on medium speed until a soft, slightly sticky dough has formed. Add a little more flour if the dough seems too sticky.

Turn the dough out onto a lightly floured work surface and pat it into a disk. Divide it in half. Lightly moisten your hands with water and gently roll one portion of dough into a rough oval. Place it lengthwise on one half of the baking sheet and use your hands and fingers to stretch and pat the dough into a log about 2 in/5 cm wide and 14 in/35 cm long. Shape the second piece of dough in the same way, moistening your hands as necessary. Press down on the logs to flatten them out a bit and make the tops even.

CONT'D

ASSA DI CIOCCOLATO BIANCO
GLASSA DI CIOCCOLATO
DI CIOC
TE VERDE CON
TO BIANCO TE VERDE CON GLASSA DI
TE VERDE CON GLASSA
CIOCCOLA
DI CIOCCOLATO BIANCO TE VERDE CON
TE VERDE CON GLASSA DI
CON
LATO
ERDE CON GLASSA DI CIOCCOLATO

4 OZ/115 G WHITE
CHOCOLATE, CHOPPED

¼ CUP/60 ML
HALF-AND-HALF
OR MILK

⅔ CUP/70 G
CONFECTIONERS' SUGAR

MAKES ABOUT 30 BISCOTTI

Bake the logs for 20 to 25 minutes, or until they are lightly browned and just set—they should be springy to the touch and there should be cracks on the surface. Transfer the baking sheet to a cooling rack. Gently slide an offset spatula under each log to loosen it from the baking sheet. Let the logs cool for 5 minutes, and then transfer them to the rack and let cool for 20 minutes. Lower the oven temperature to 300°F/150°C.

Transfer the cooled logs to a cutting board and, using a Santoku knife or a serrated bread knife, cut them on the diagonal into 1-in-/2.5-cm-thick slices. Arrange the slices, cut-side up, on the baking sheet (in batches if necessary) and bake for 10 minutes. Turn the slices over and bake for another 10 minutes, until they are crisp. Transfer the slices to the rack to cool completely.

Place the rack over a rimmed baking sheet or a sheet of wax paper. Arrange the slices upright on the rack. Put the white chocolate and half-and-half in a microwave-safe bowl. Microwave at 50 percent power in 30-second intervals, stirring after each interval, until the chocolate has completely melted. Whisk in ¼ cup/20 g of the confectioners' sugar all at once, whisking vigorously to make sure the mixture is well combined and no lumps remain. The glaze should be smooth and thick, but still loose enough to fall from the tip of the whisk in a ribbon. Add the remaining confectioners' sugar if the glaze seems too thin.

Dip the tip of the whisk or a fork into the icing and drizzle the ribbon of icing back and forth over the biscotti. Place the baking sheet in the refrigerator for 30 minutes for the glaze to set. Let the biscotti return to room temperature before serving. The biscotti will keep for up to 10 days in an airtight container stored at room temperature.

WHAT TO DRINK: A cup of hot, unsweetened green tea.

SPICED AND ICED
GINGER

You'll want to share these crunchy biscotti infused with warm holiday spices—cinnamon, cloves, mace, nutmeg, and, most prominent, ginger. Pack them in cellophane bags tied with festive ribbons and give them to your favorite cookie lovers.

Heat the oven to 350°F/180°C. Lightly coat an 11-by-17-in/ 28-by-43-cm rimmed baking sheet with the 1 Tbsp oil.

Combine the flour, granulated sugar, brown sugar, baking powder, ground ginger, cinnamon, cloves, mace, nutmeg, and salt in the bowl of a stand mixer fitted with the paddle attachment. Mix briefly on low speed. Add the almonds and mix on low to combine. Add the eggs and 2 Tbsp of the grated fresh ginger and mix on medium speed until a soft, slightly sticky dough has formed. Drizzle in a few drops of oil if necessary to make the dough come together.

Turn the dough out onto a lightly floured work surface and pat it into a disk. Divide it in half. Lightly moisten your hands with water and gently roll one portion of dough into a rough oval. Place it lengthwise on one half of the baking sheet and use your hands and fingers to stretch and pat the dough into a log about 2½ in/6 cm wide and 12 in/30 cm long. Shape the second piece of dough in the same way, moistening your hands as necessary. Press down on the logs to flatten them out a bit and make the tops even.

Bake the logs for 25 minutes, or until they are lightly browned and just set—they should be springy to the touch and there should be cracks on the surface. Transfer the baking sheet to a cooling rack. Gently slide an offset spatula under each log to

★

1 TBSP VEGETABLE OIL, PLUS A FEW DROPS IF NEEDED

2 CUPS/255 G UNBLEACHED ALL-PURPOSE FLOUR

½ CUP/100 G GRANULATED SUGAR

½ CUP/100 G LIGHTLY PACKED LIGHT BROWN SUGAR

1 TSP BAKING POWDER

2 TSP GROUND GINGER

½ TSP GROUND CINNAMON

½ TSP GROUND CLOVES

PINCH OF GROUND MACE

PINCH OF FRESHLY GRATED NUTMEG

¼ TSP FINE SEA SALT

¾ CUP/105 G WHOLE ALMONDS, TOASTED (SEE PAGE 16)

CONT'D

2 LARGE EGGS,
LIGHTLY BEATEN

5 TBSP/10 G FINELY
GRATED PEELED
FRESH GINGER

1 CUP/100 G
CONFECTIONERS' SUGAR

A FEW DROPS OF
HALF-AND-HALF OR
MILK, AS NEEDED

MAKES **32** TO **34** BISCOTTI

loosen it from the baking sheet. Let the logs cool for 5 minutes, and then transfer them to the rack and let cool for 20 minutes. Lower the oven temperature to 300°F/150°C.

Transfer the cooled logs to a cutting board and, using a Santoku knife or a serrated bread knife, cut them on the diagonal into ½-in-/12-mm-thick slices. Arrange the slices, cut-side up, on the baking sheet (in batches if necessary) and bake for 12 minutes. Turn the slices over and bake for another 12 minutes, until they are crisp. Transfer the slices to the rack to cool completely.

Place the rack over a rimmed baking sheet or a sheet of wax paper. Arrange the slices cut-side up on the rack. Put the remaining 3 Tbsp grated ginger into a small fine-mesh sieve. Hold the sieve over a small bowl and press the grated ginger with your fingers or the back of a spoon. Measure out 1 Tbsp of the ginger juice.

In a small bowl, whisk together the confectioners' sugar and ginger juice. Dribble in as much half-and-half as needed to make the icing smooth and opaque but still loose enough to fall from the tip of the whisk in a ribbon.

Dip the tip of the whisk or a fork into the icing and drizzle the ribbon of icing back and forth over the biscotti. Let the icing dry completely before serving. The biscotti will keep for up to 10 days in an airtight container stored at room temperature.

WHAT TO DRINK: A glass of sparkling, sweet Moscato d'Asti.

HONEY WHOLE-WHEAT

★

1 TBSP VEGETABLE OIL

1½ TO 2 CUPS/185 TO
255 G WHOLE-WHEAT
FLOUR

½ CUP/60 G UNBLEACHED
ALL-PURPOSE FLOUR

½ CUP/100 G
LIGHTLY PACKED DARK
BROWN SUGAR

1 TSP BAKING POWDER

¼ TSP FINE SEA SALT

½ CUP/70 G HAZELNUTS,
TOASTED AND SKINNED
(SEE PAGE 16)

¼ CUP/35 G BLANCHED
(PEELED) WHOLE ALMONDS,
TOASTED (SEE PAGE 16)

Although I love whole wheat in breads, I was never keen on whole-wheat sweets. That changed when I made these biscotti. They are surprisingly light in texture—crispy and a little crumbly. The toasty flavor of the whole wheat is enhanced by the rich, warm flavor of the nuts and the sweetness of the sultanas.

Heat the oven to 350°F/180°C. Lightly coat an 11-by-17-in/28-by-43-cm rimmed baking sheet with the oil.

Combine 1½ cups/185 g of the whole-wheat flour, the all-purpose flour, brown sugar, baking powder, and salt in the bowl of a stand mixer fitted with the paddle attachment. Mix briefly on low speed. Add the hazelnuts, almonds, and sultanas and mix briefly on low to combine. Add the butter in pieces and mix on medium-low speed until the mixture looks like damp sand.

In a small bowl, whisk together the eggs and honey. Pour the egg mixture into the dry mixture and mix on medium speed until a soft, slightly sticky dough has formed. Sprinkle in a little more whole-wheat flour if the dough seems too loose or sticky.

Turn the dough out onto a lightly floured work surface and pat it into a disk. Divide it in half. Lightly moisten your hands with water and gently roll one portion of dough into a rough oval. Place it lengthwise on one half of the baking sheet and use your hands and fingers to stretch and pat the dough into a log about 2 in/5 cm wide and 12 in/30 cm long. Shape the second piece of dough in the same way, moistening your hands as necessary. Press down on the logs to flatten them out a bit and make the tops even.

Bake the logs for 25 to 28 minutes, or until they are lightly browned and just set—they should be springy to the touch and there should be cracks on the surface. Transfer the baking sheet to a cooling rack. Gently slide an offset spatula under each log to loosen it from the baking sheet. Let the logs cool for 5 minutes, and then transfer them to the rack and let cool for 20 minutes. Lower the oven temperature to 300°F/150°C.

Transfer the cooled logs to a cutting board and, using a Santoku knife or a serrated bread knife, cut them on the diagonal into ⅔-in-/15-mm-thick slices. Arrange the slices, cut-side up, on the baking sheet (in batches if necessary) and bake for 10 minutes. Turn the slices over and bake for another 10 minutes, until they are crisp and golden brown. Transfer the slices to the rack to cool completely. The biscotti will keep for up to 10 days in an airtight container stored at room temperature.

WHAT TO DRINK: A glass of sherry.

★

⅔ CUP/115 G SULTANAS
(GOLDEN RAISINS)

4 TBSP/55 G UNSALTED
BUTTER, CUT INTO
½-IN/12-MM PIECES, AT
COOL ROOM TEMPERATURE

2 LARGE EGGS,
LIGHTLY BEATEN

1 TBSP HONEY

MAKES ABOUT 36 BISCOTTI

WALNUT
AND
SPELT

★

1 TBSP VEGETABLE OIL

2 CUPS PLUS 2 TBSP/
240 G WHOLE-GRAIN
SPELT FLOUR
(SEE PAGE 14)

1 CUP/200 G
TURBINADO SUGAR,
PLUS SCANT 4 TSP

1 TSP BAKING POWDER

¼ TSP FINE SEA SALT

FINELY GRATED ZEST OF
2 ORGANIC LEMONS

2 CUPS/230 G COARSELY
CHOPPED WALNUTS,
TOASTED (SEE PAGE 16)

2 LARGE EGGS,
LIGHTLY BEATEN

My friend Maria Speck is an accomplished baker and the award-winning author of the book Ancient Grains for Modern Meals. *When I asked if she would like to contribute a recipe to this book she outdid herself, coming up with this spectacular whole-grain cookie. Here's what she says about it: "These rustic biscotti, chock-full with toasted walnuts, are made with whole-grain spelt flour, an ancient wheat variety traditionally used in many parts of Europe. Spelt flour adds a subtle nuttiness and sublime texture to these lemon-infused treats—no wonder it is having a huge comeback." Look for spelt flour at natural foods stores or online.*

Heat the oven to 350°F/180°C. Lightly coat an 11-by-17-in/ 28-by-43-cm rimmed baking sheet with the vegetable oil.

Combine the spelt flour, 1 cup/200 g sugar, baking powder, salt, and lemon zest in the bowl of a stand mixer fitted with the paddle attachment. Add the walnuts and mix on low speed to combine. In a separate bowl, gently whisk together the eggs, olive oil, limoncello, and vanilla. Pour the egg mixture into the flour mixture and mix on medium speed until a soft, slightly sticky dough has formed. Cover the bowl with a plate or with plastic wrap and set aside for 25 to 30 minutes; this allows the spelt to soften for a more appealing texture.

Turn the dough out onto a lightly floured work surface and pat it into a disk. Divide it into quarters. Lightly moisten your hands with water and gently roll one portion of dough into a rough oval. Place it crosswise on the baking sheet and use your hands and fingers to stretch and pat the dough into a log about 1½ in/4 cm wide and 9 in/23 cm long. Shape the remaining pieces of dough in the same way, moistening your hands as necessary, leaving at least 2 in/5 cm between the logs. Press down on the logs to flatten them out a bit and make the tops even. Sprinkle each log with a scant 1 tsp of the remaining sugar.

Bake the logs for 25 minutes, or until they are lightly browned and just set—they should be springy to the touch and there should be cracks on the surface. Transfer the baking sheet to a cooling rack. Gently slide an offset spatula under each log to loosen it from the baking sheet. Let the logs cool for 5 minutes, and then transfer them to the rack and let cool for 20 minutes. Lower the oven temperature to 300°F/150°C.

Transfer the cooled logs to a cutting board and, using a Santoku knife or a serrated bread knife, cut them on the diagonal into ½-in-/12-mm-thick slices. Arrange the slices, cut-side up, on the baking sheet (in batches if necessary) and bake for 15 minutes. Turn the slices over and bake for another 15 minutes, until they are crisp and emit a lovely toasty scent. Transfer the slices to the rack to cool completely. The biscotti will keep for up to 10 days in an airtight container stored at room temperature.

WHAT TO DRINK: Vin Santo or a glass of nocino, a walnut-flavored liqueur from Emilia-Romagna.

★

½ CUP/120 ML EXTRA-VIRGIN OLIVE OIL

1 TBSP LIMONCELLO OR BRANDY

1 TSP PURE VANILLA EXTRACT

MAKES ABOUT
62
SMALL BISCOTTI

THE SAVORY SIDE

CRISPY
PANCETTA

★

1 TBSP VEGETABLE OIL

4 OZ/115 G PANCETTA,
CUT INTO ¼-IN/6-MM
DICE

2 CUPS/255 G
UNBLEACHED
ALL-PURPOSE FLOUR

1 TSP BAKING POWDER

1 TSP COARSELY GROUND
BLACK PEPPER

½ TSP FINE SEA SALT

1 CUP/85 G GRATED
PECORINO ROMANO CHEESE

½ CUP/40 G GRATED
PARMIGIANO-REGGIANO
CHEESE

½ CUP/50 G SLICED
ALMONDS, TOASTED
(SEE PAGE 16)

Every once in a while, my mom would make a trip to the Italian bakery in Trenton, New Jersey, where she would pick up (among many things) a delicious ring loaf of bread studded with crispy bits of pancetta and savory with tangy cheese. That's what I had in mind when I created this recipe.

Heat the oven to 350°F/180°C. Lightly coat an 11-by-17-in/ 28-by-43-cm rimmed baking sheet with the oil.

Put the pancetta in a cold cast-iron or heavy-bottomed skillet and set it over medium heat. Cook, stirring once or twice, until the pancetta begins to sizzle. Turn the heat to medium-low and cook, stirring a few times, for about 10 minutes, or until the pancetta has rendered some of its fat and is crisp. Turn the heat to low if necessary to keep the pancetta from burning. Using a slotted spoon, transfer the pancetta pieces to a paper towel–lined plate to cool. Reserve 1 Tbsp of the rendered fat.

Combine the flour, baking powder, pepper, and salt in the bowl of a stand mixer fitted with the paddle attachment. Mix briefly on low speed. Add the Pecorino Romano, Parmigiano-Reggiano, almonds, and cooled pancetta and mix on low to combine. Add the reserved pancetta fat and the butter in pieces and mix on medium-low speed until the mixture looks like damp sand. Add the eggs and wine and mix on medium speed until a soft, slightly sticky dough has formed.

Turn the dough out onto a lightly floured work surface and pat it into a disk. Divide it into quarters. Lightly moisten your hands with water and gently roll one portion of dough into a rough oval. Place it crosswise on the baking sheet and use your hands and fingers to stretch and pat the dough into

CONT'D

4 TBSP/55 G UNSALTED
BUTTER, CUT INTO
½-IN/12-MM PIECES, AT
COOL ROOM TEMPERATURE

2 LARGE EGGS,
LIGHTLY BEATEN

2 TBSP DRY WHITE WINE,
HALF-AND-HALF, OR MILK

MAKES ABOUT 44 BISCOTTI

a log about 1½ in/4 cm wide and 9 in/23 cm long. Shape the remaining pieces of dough in the same way, moistening your hands as necessary, leaving at least 2 in/5 cm between the logs. Press down on the logs to flatten them out a bit and make the tops even.

Bake the logs for 25 minutes, or until they are lightly browned and just set—they should be springy to the touch and there should be cracks on the surface. Transfer the baking sheet to a cooling rack. Gently slide an offset spatula under each log to loosen it from the baking sheet. Let the logs cool for 5 minutes, and then transfer them to the rack and let cool for 20 minutes. Lower the oven temperature to 300°F/150°C.

Transfer the cooled logs to a cutting board and, using a Santoku knife or a serrated bread knife, cut them on the diagonal into ½-in-/12-mm-thick slices. Arrange the slices, cut-side up, on the baking sheet (in batches if necessary) and bake for 20 minutes. Turn the slices over and bake for another 15 to 20 minutes, until they are crisp and golden. Transfer the slices to the rack to cool completely. The biscotti will keep for up to 10 days in an airtight container stored at room temperature.

WHAT TO DRINK: Pecorino (the wine, not the cheese) or your favorite dry white wine.

MOUNTAIN GORGONZOLA

AND WALNUT

No doubt you'll laugh when I tell you that the inspiration for these biscotti came from that buffet table classic—the holiday cheese ball. But I also have no doubt that after one bite, you'll be won over. Crispy, buttery, and rich with tangy blue cheese flavor, these biscotti are perfect for a holiday gathering.

Heat the oven to 350°F/180°C. Lightly coat an 11-by-17-in/ 28-by-43-cm rimmed baking sheet with the oil.

Combine the flour, baking powder, salt, pepper, and walnuts in the bowl of a stand mixer fitted with the paddle attachment. Mix briefly on low speed. Add the Gorgonzola in pieces and mix briefly to combine. Add the butter in pieces and mix on medium-low speed until the mixture looks like damp sand. Pour in the eggs and mix on medium speed until a soft, slightly sticky dough has formed.

Turn the dough out onto a lightly floured work surface and pat it into a disk. Divide it in half. Lightly moisten your hands with water and gently roll one portion of dough into a rough oval. Place it lengthwise on one half of the baking sheet and use your hands and fingers to stretch and pat the dough into a log about 2½ in/6 cm wide and 12 in/30 cm long. Shape the second piece of dough in the same way, moistening your hands as necessary. Press down on the logs to flatten them out a bit and make the tops even.

CONT'D

1 TBSP VEGETABLE OIL

2 CUPS/255 G UNBLEACHED ALL-PURPOSE FLOUR

1 TSP BAKING POWDER

½ TSP FINE SEA SALT

½ TSP FRESHLY GROUND BLACK PEPPER

½ CUP/55 G FINELY CHOPPED WALNUTS

5 OZ/140 G MOUNTAIN GORGONZOLA (ALSO KNOWN AS GORGONZOLA PICCANTE), CRUMBLED

4 TBSP/55 G UNSALTED BUTTER, CUT INTO ½-IN/12-MM PIECES, AT COOL ROOM TEMPERATURE

2 LARGE EGGS, LIGHTLY BEATEN

MAKES ABOUT **36** BISCOTTI

Bake the logs for 25 minutes, or until they are lightly browned and just set—they should be springy to the touch and there should be cracks on the surface. Transfer the baking sheet to a cooling rack. Gently slide an offset spatula under each log to loosen it from the baking sheet. Let the logs cool for 5 minutes, and then transfer them to the rack and let cool for 20 minutes. Lower the oven temperature to 300°F/150°C.

Transfer the cooled logs to a cutting board and, using a Santoku knife or a serrated bread knife, cut them on the diagonal into ⅓-in-/8-mm-thick slices. Arrange the slices, cut-side up, on the baking sheet (in batches if necessary) and bake for 15 minutes. Turn the slices over and bake for another 15 minutes, or until they are crisp and golden. Transfer the slices to the rack to cool completely. The biscotti will keep for up to 10 days in an airtight container stored at room temperature.

WHAT TO DRINK: A dry red wine such as Barbaresco or Barbera.

ALMOND

AND

AGED ASIAGO

★

1 TBSP VEGETABLE OIL

2 CUPS/255 G
UNBLEACHED
ALL-PURPOSE FLOUR

1 TSP BAKING POWDER

1 TSP FINE SEA SALT

2 TSP COARSELY GROUND
BLACK PEPPER

HEAPING 1 CUP/90 G
GRATED AGED
ASIAGO CHEESE

½ CUP/50 G
SLICED ALMONDS

6 TBSP/85 G UNSALTED
BUTTER, CUT INTO
½-IN/12-MM PIECES, AT
COOL ROOM TEMPERATURE

Crispy, buttery, and infused with the sharp aroma of Asiago cheese, these salty biscuits belong on an antipasto platter together with cracked green olives and good-quality, thinly sliced salami and prosciutto.

Heat the oven to 350°F/180°C. Lightly coat an 11-by-17-in/28-by-43-cm rimmed baking sheet with the oil.

Combine the flour, baking powder, salt, and pepper in the bowl of a stand mixer fitted with the paddle attachment. Mix briefly on low speed. Add the cheese and almonds and mix briefly on low to combine. Add the butter in pieces and mix on medium-low speed until the mixture looks like damp sand. Set aside 1 Tbsp of the beaten eggs. Combine the remaining eggs with 2 Tbsp milk and pour into the mixing bowl. Mix on medium speed until a soft, slightly sticky dough has formed. Add the remaining milk if necessary to make the dough come together.

Turn the dough out onto a lightly floured work surface and pat it into a disk. Divide it in half. Lightly moisten your hands with water and gently roll one portion of dough into a rough oval. Place it lengthwise on one half of the baking sheet and use your hands and fingers to stretch and pat the dough into a log about 2½ in/6 cm wide and 12 in/30 cm long. Shape the second piece of dough in the same way, moistening your hands as necessary. Press down on the logs to flatten them out a bit and make the tops even. Brush the reserved egg over the tops of the logs.

Bake the logs for 25 to 30 minutes, or until they are lightly browned and just set—they should be springy to the touch and there should be cracks on the surface. Transfer the baking sheet to a cooling rack. Gently slide an offset spatula under each log to loosen it from the baking sheet. Let the logs cool for 5 minutes, and then transfer them to the rack and let cool for 20 minutes. Lower the oven temperature to 300°F/150°C.

Transfer the cooled logs to a cutting board and, using a Santoku knife or a serrated bread knife, cut them on the diagonal into ⅓-in-/8-mm-thick slices. Arrange the slices, cut-side up, on the baking sheet (in batches if necessary) and bake for 20 minutes. Turn the slices over and bake for another 15 to 20 minutes, until they are crisp and golden. Transfer the slices to the rack to cool completely. The biscotti will keep for up to 10 days in an airtight container stored at room temperature.

WHAT TO DRINK: A glass of chilled Prosecco.

★

2 LARGE EGGS, LIGHTLY BEATEN

2 TO 4 TBSP WHOLE MILK

MAKES ABOUT **45** BISCOTTI

PEPPER JACK

AND GREEN PEPPERCORN

★

1 TBSP VEGETABLE OIL

2 CUPS/255 G
UNBLEACHED
ALL-PURPOSE FLOUR

1 TSP BAKING POWDER

1 TSP FINE SEA SALT

1 TBSP CRUSHED OR
COARSELY GROUND
GREEN PEPPERCORNS
(SEE HEADNOTE)

HEAPING 1 CUP/125 G
GRATED PEPPER JACK
CHEESE

¾ CUP/60 G
SLICED ALMONDS

4 TBSP/55 G UNSALTED
BUTTER, CUT INTO
½-IN/12-MM PIECES, AT
COOL ROOM TEMPERATURE

The subtle flecks of red and green make these biscotti a nice choice for a holiday antipasto platter. Pepper Jack might not be the most sophisticated cheese to come out of California, but it has a buttery texture and a zesty appeal from the bits of jalapeño and habanero chile mixed in. Crushed green peppercorns give the biscotti an additional kick. To crush green peppercorns, put them in a resealable sandwich bag and pound them (gently) with a flat, heavy object such as the bottom of a heavy skillet— I use a cast-iron skillet—or a meat tenderizer.

Heat the oven to 350°F/180°C. Lightly coat an 11-by-17-in/ 28-by-43-cm rimmed baking sheet with the oil.

Combine the flour, baking powder, salt, and peppercorns in the bowl of a stand mixer fitted with the paddle attachment. Mix briefly on low speed. Add the cheese and almonds and mix briefly on low to combine. Add the butter in pieces and mix on medium-low speed until the mixture looks like damp sand. Set aside 1 Tbsp of the beaten eggs. Combine the remaining eggs with 2 Tbsp half-and-half and pour into the mixing bowl. Mix on medium speed until a soft, slightly sticky dough has formed. Add the remaining half-and-half if necessary to make the dough come together.

Turn the dough out onto a lightly floured work surface and pat it into a disk. Divide it in half. Lightly moisten your hands with water and gently roll one portion of dough into a rough oval. Place it lengthwise on one half of the baking sheet and use your hands and fingers to stretch and pat the dough into a log about 2½ in/6 cm wide and 12 in/30 cm long. Shape the second piece of dough in the same way, moistening your hands as

CONT'D

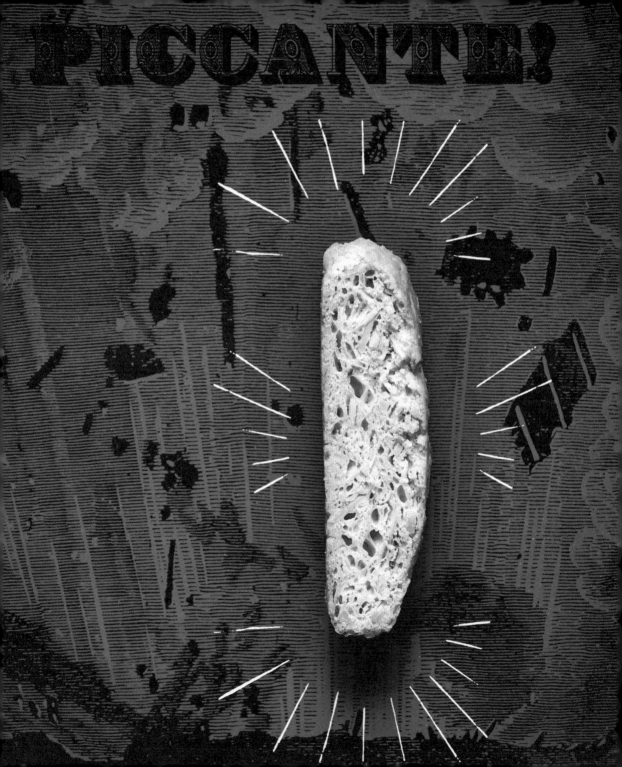

2 LARGE EGGS,
LIGHTLY BEATEN

2 TO 4 TBSP
HALF-AND-HALF OR MILK

★

MAKES **28** TO **30** BISCOTTI

necessary. Press down on the logs to flatten them out a bit and make the tops even. Brush the reserved egg over the tops of the logs.

Bake the logs for 25 to 30 minutes, or until they are lightly browned and just set—they should be springy to the touch and there should be cracks on the surface. Transfer the baking sheet to a cooling rack. Gently slide an offset spatula under each log to loosen it from the baking sheet. Let the logs cool for 5 minutes, and then transfer them to the rack and let cool for 20 minutes. Lower the oven temperature to 325°F/165°C.

Transfer the cooled logs to a cutting board and, using a Santoku knife or a serrated bread knife, cut them on the diagonal into ½-in-/12-mm-thick slices. Arrange the slices, cut-side up, on the baking sheet (in batches if necessary) and bake for 20 minutes. Turn the slices over and bake for another 15 to 20 minutes, until they are crisp and golden. Transfer the slices to the rack to cool completely. The biscotti will keep for up to 10 days in an airtight container stored at room temperature.

WHAT TO DRINK: Two Hearted Ale from Bell's Brewery—or crack open your favorite cold brew.

SMOKY
GOUDA

Smoked paprika may not be Italian, but it's one of my favorite savory spices. I love it sprinkled on roasted potatoes, in egg salad, in soups and stews, and in these fragrant biscotti. I wanted to underline that smoky flavor, so I added a generous quantity of smoked Gouda cheese to the mix.

Heat the oven to 350°F/180° C. Lightly coat an 11-by-17-in/ 28-by-43-cm rimmed baking sheet with the vegetable oil.

Combine the all-purpose flour, whole-wheat flour, baking powder, salt, sweet paprika, and smoked paprika in the bowl of a stand mixer fitted with the paddle attachment. Mix briefly on low speed. Add the pecans and mix to combine and to break up the nuts into small pieces. Add the cheese and mix briefly on low to combine. Add the butter in pieces and mix on medium-low speed until the mixture looks like damp sand. Set aside 1 Tbsp of the beaten eggs. Combine the remaining eggs with the olive oil and milk and pour into the mixing bowl. Mix on medium speed until a soft, slightly sticky dough has formed.

Turn the dough out onto a lightly floured work surface and pat it into a disk. Divide it in half. Lightly moisten your hands with water and gently roll one portion of dough into a rough oval. Place it lengthwise on one half of the baking sheet and use your hands and fingers to stretch and pat the dough into a log about 2½ in/6 cm wide and 12 in/30 cm long. Shape the second piece of dough in the same way, moistening your hands as necessary. Press down on the logs to flatten them out a bit and make the tops even. Brush the reserved egg over the tops of the logs.

CONT'D

★

1 TBSP VEGETABLE OIL

1½ CUPS/185 G UNBLEACHED ALL-PURPOSE FLOUR

½ CUP/60 G WHOLE-WHEAT FLOUR

1 TSP BAKING POWDER

1 TSP FINE SEA SALT

½ TSP SWEET HUNGARIAN PAPRIKA

¼ TSP SMOKED PAPRIKA (PIMENTÓN)

½ CUP/55 G PECAN HALVES

1 CUP/115 G GRATED SMOKED GOUDA CHEESE

4 TBSP/55 G UNSALTED BUTTER, CUT INTO ½-IN/12-MM PIECES, AT COOL ROOM TEMPERATURE

2 LARGE EGGS,
LIGHTLY BEATEN

2 TBSP EXTRA-VIRGIN
OLIVE OIL

2 TBSP MILK OR
HALF-AND-HALF

MAKES ABOUT **30** BISCOTTI

Bake the logs for 25 to 30 minutes, or until they are lightly browned and just set—they should be springy to the touch and there should be cracks on the surface. Transfer the baking sheet to a cooling rack. Gently slide an offset spatula under each log to loosen it from the baking sheet. Let the logs cool for 5 minutes, and then transfer them to the rack and let cool for 20 minutes. Lower the oven temperature to 325°F/165°C.

Transfer the cooled logs to a cutting board and, using a Santoku knife or a serrated bread knife, cut them on the diagonal into ½-in-/12-mm-thick slices. Arrange the slices, cut-side up, on the baking sheet (in batches if necessary) and bake for 20 minutes. Turn the slices over and bake for another 15 to 20 minutes, until they are crisp and golden. Transfer the slices to the rack to cool completely. The biscotti will keep for up to 10 days in an airtight container stored at room temperature.

WHAT TO DRINK: Dolcetto di Dogliani, a smoky red wine from Piedmont, if you can find it. Otherwise, Dolcetto d'Alba.

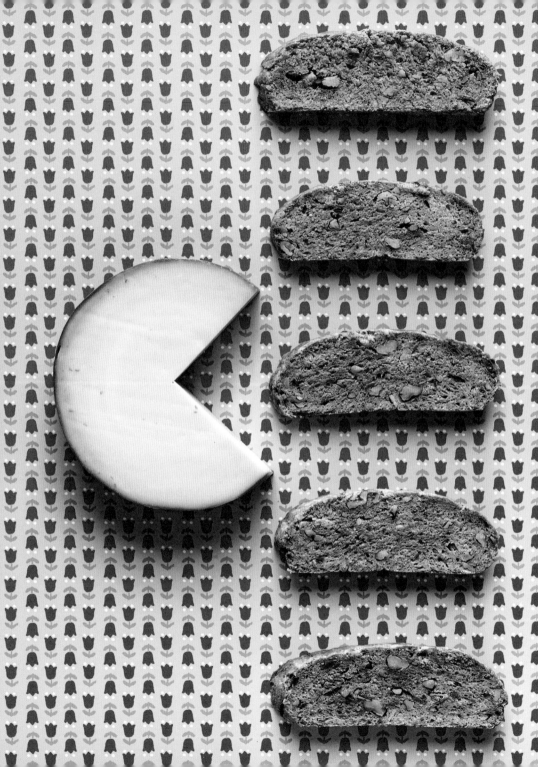

CORNMEAL WITH
ROSEMARY
AND
PARMIGIANO

★

1 TBSP VEGETABLE OIL

1½ CUPS/185 G
UNBLEACHED
ALL-PURPOSE FLOUR

½ CUP/70 G
FINE CORNMEAL

1 TSP BAKING POWDER

¼ TSP FINE SEA SALT

1 CUP/80 G GRATED
PARMIGIANO-REGGIANO
CHEESE

1 CUP/100 G SLICED
ALMONDS, TOASTED
(SEE PAGE 16)

1 TBSP FINELY MINCED
FRESH ROSEMARY

6 TBSP/85 G UNSALTED
BUTTER, CUT INTO
½-IN/12-MM PIECES, AT
COOL ROOM TEMPERATURE

Fine-ground cornmeal adds a delicate crunch and pretty golden hue to these rosemary-infused biscotti. Slice these thinly and serve them with a nice runny cheese.

Heat the oven to 350°F/180°C. Lightly coat an 11-by-17-in/ 28-by-43-cm rimmed baking sheet with the oil.

Combine the flour, cornmeal, baking powder, and salt in the bowl of a stand mixer fitted with the paddle attachment. Mix briefly on low speed. Add the cheese, almonds, and rosemary and mix to combine. Add the butter in pieces and mix on medium-low speed until the mixture looks like damp sand. Set aside 1 Tbsp of the beaten eggs. Combine the remaining eggs with 2 Tbsp half-and-half and pour into the mixing bowl. Mix on medium speed until a soft, slightly sticky dough has formed. Add the remaining half-and-half if necessary to make the dough come together.

Turn the dough out onto a lightly floured work surface and pat it into a disk. Divide it in half. Lightly moisten your hands with water and gently roll one portion of dough into a rough oval. Place it lengthwise on one half of the baking sheet and use your hands and fingers to stretch and pat the dough into a log about 2½ in/6 cm wide and 12 in/30 cm long. Shape the second piece of dough in the same way, moistening your hands as necessary. Press down on the logs to flatten them out a bit and make the tops even. Brush the reserved egg over the tops of the logs.

Bake the logs for 25 to 30 minutes, or until they are lightly browned and just set—they should be springy to the touch and there should be cracks on the surface. Transfer the baking sheet to a cooling rack. Gently slide an offset spatula under each log to loosen it from the baking sheet. Let the logs cool for 5 minutes, and then transfer them to the rack and let cool for 20 minutes. Lower the oven temperature to 300°F/150°C.

Transfer the cooled logs to a cutting board and, using a Santoku knife or a serrated bread knife, cut them on the diagonal into ⅓-in-/8-mm-thick slices. Arrange the slices, cut-side up, on the baking sheet (in batches if necessary) and bake for 20 minutes. Turn the slices over and bake for another 15 to 20 minutes, until they are crisp and golden. Transfer the slices to the rack to cool completely. The biscotti will keep for up to 10 days in an airtight container stored at room temperature.

WHAT TO DRINK: Chianti Classico.

★

2 LARGE EGGS, LIGHTLY BEATEN

2 TO 4 TBSP HALF-AND-HALF OR MILK

MAKES ABOUT BISCOTTI

SUN-DRIED TOMATO

AND FENNEL

---⭐---

1 TBSP VEGETABLE OIL

2 CUPS/255 G
UNBLEACHED
ALL-PURPOSE FLOUR

1 TSP BAKING POWDER

1 TSP FINE SEA SALT

1 TSP COARSELY GROUND
BLACK PEPPER

1 TBSP WHOLE FENNEL
SEEDS, LIGHTLY TOASTED
(SEE PAGE 16)

HEAPING 1 CUP/90 G
GRATED IBERICO CHEESE

½ CUP/50 G SLICED
ALMONDS, TOASTED
(SEE PAGE 16)

⅓ CUP/30 G PACKED
COARSELY CHOPPED
SUN-DRIED TOMATOES
(NOT OIL-PACKED)

Inspiration struck one day when I spied a wedge of tangy Iberico cheese—made in Spain from a blend of cow's, goat's, and sheep's milk—in my fridge. I mixed it into the biscotti dough along with chopped sun-dried tomatoes and toasted fennel seeds, and these piquant cookies were born. They are diminutive in size and big in flavor, which makes them perfect for a cocktail party.

Heat the oven to 350°F/180°C. Lightly coat an 11-by-17-in/28-by-43-cm rimmed baking sheet with the oil.

Combine the flour, baking powder, salt, pepper, and fennel seeds in the bowl of a stand mixer fitted with the paddle attachment. Mix briefly on low speed. Add the cheese, almonds, and sun-dried tomatoes and mix to combine. Add the butter in pieces and mix on medium-low speed until the mixture looks like damp sand. Add the eggs and half-and-half and mix on medium speed until a soft, slightly sticky dough has formed.

Turn the dough out onto a lightly floured work surface and pat it into a disk. Divide it into quarters. Lightly moisten your hands with water and gently roll one portion of dough into a rough oval. Place it crosswise on the baking sheet and use your hands and fingers to stretch and pat the dough into a log about 1½ in/4 cm wide and 9 in/23 cm long. Shape the remaining pieces of dough in the same way, moistening your hands as necessary, leaving at least 2 in/5 cm between the logs. Press down on the logs to flatten them out a bit and make the tops even.

Bake the logs for 25 minutes, or until they are lightly browned and just set—they should be springy to the touch and there should be cracks on the surface. Transfer the baking sheet to a cooling rack. Gently slide an offset spatula under each log to loosen it from the baking sheet. Let the logs cool for 5 minutes, and then transfer them to the rack and let cool for 20 minutes. Lower the oven temperature to 300°F/150°C.

Transfer the cooled logs to a cutting board and, using a Santoku knife or a serrated bread knife, cut them on the diagonal into ⅝-in-/15-mm-thick slices. Arrange the slices, cut-side up, on the baking sheet (in batches if necessary) and bake for 20 minutes. Turn the slices over and bake for another 15 to 20 minutes, until they are crisp and golden. Transfer the slices to the rack to cool completely. The biscotti will keep for up to 10 days in an airtight container stored at room temperature.

WHAT TO DRINK: A white Rioja.

★

4 TBSP/55 G UNSALTED
BUTTER, CUT INTO
½-IN/12-MM PIECES, AT
COOL ROOM TEMPERATURE

2 LARGE EGGS,
LIGHTLY BEATEN

2 TBSP HALF-AND-HALF
OR MILK

MAKES ABOUT **40** BISCOTTI

BEYOND
BISCOTTI

HAZELNUT BUTTER RINGS

★

¼ CUP/35 G HAZELNUTS, TOASTED AND SKINNED (SEE PAGE 16), PLUS AN ADDITIONAL HANDFUL FOR GARNISHING THE COOKIES

1¾ CUPS/215 G UNBLEACHED ALL-PURPOSE FLOUR

½ TSP FINE SEA SALT

8 TBSP/115 G UNSALTED BUTTER, CUT INTO ½-IN/12-MM PIECES, AT COOL ROOM TEMPERATURE

⅔ CUP/70 G CONFECTIONERS' SUGAR

2 LARGE EGGS, SEPARATED

1 TBSP HAZELNUT OIL OR OLIVE OIL

MAKES ABOUT 32 COOKIES

Hovering somewhere between a traditional butter cookie and shortbread, these pretty rings are subtly flavored with ground toasted hazelnuts and decorated with a single whole nut. Definitely worthy of your holiday cookie tray.

Place the ¼ cup/35 g hazelnuts in the work bowl of a food processor fitted with the metal blade and process until the nuts are finely ground, but not so fine that they begin to turn into a paste. Transfer the ground nuts to a medium bowl and add the flour and salt. Whisk to combine.

In a stand mixer fitted with the paddle attachment, beat the butter and confectioners' sugar on medium speed until thoroughly combined. Beat in the egg yolks and hazelnut oil. Add the flour-hazelnut mixture and beat on low speed until incorporated. Scrape the dough onto a sheet of wax paper, wrap tightly, and refrigerate overnight or until thoroughly chilled.

Heat the oven to 325°F/165°C. Remove the dough from the refrigerator and cut it into quarters. Pinch off pieces of dough about the size of a small walnut. Roll each piece into a thin rope about 4 in/10 cm long. Bring the ends together to form a ring about 2 in/5 cm in diameter. Pinch the ends to seal. Set the cookies on an ungreased rimmed baking sheet.

Lightly beat the egg whites. Using a pastry brush or your finger, brush a little egg white onto the spot where you sealed each ring. Gently press a whole hazelnut into the seal.

CONT'D

Bake the cookies for 15 to 20 minutes, until set and just barely browned. Let the cookies cool on the baking sheet for 5 minutes, and then use an offset spatula to transfer them to a cooling rack. Cool to room temperature before serving. The cookies will keep for up to 1 week in an airtight container stored at room temperature.

WHAT TO DRINK: Hazelnut liqueur such as Frangelico.

HAZELNUT MERINGUES

A trip to Pasticceria Marinari, in Rome, was always a welcome treat when I was a child. Being something of a creature of habit back then, I always got the same thing: two giant meringues drizzled with bittersweet chocolate and sandwiched together with whipped cream. Here is a slightly more restrained, more adult-friendly version of one of my favorite cookies.

Position two racks in the bottom third of the oven and heat the oven to 275°F/135°C. Line two 11-by-17-in/28-by-43-cm rimmed baking sheets with parchment paper.

Combine the egg whites and cream of tartar in the bowl of a stand mixer fitted with the whisk attachment. Beat on medium speed until foamy. Sprinkle in the salt, raise the speed to high, and beat in the sugar, 1 Tbsp at a time. Add the vanilla and beat until the egg whites hold stiff, glossy peaks that curl at the tips. Gently fold in the hazelnuts using a silicone spatula.

Drop rounded teaspoonfuls of meringue onto the baking sheets. Bake the meringues for 35 to 40 minutes, or until they are just beginning to turn pale gold. Turn off the heat and leave the meringues in the oven with the door shut for 30 minutes. (Do not open the oven door during this time.) After 30 minutes, remove the baking sheets from the oven. Use an offset spatula to gently transfer the meringues to cooling racks. Let cool completely. Reserve the parchment-lined baking sheets.

CONT'D

★

4 EGG WHITES, AT ROOM TEMPERATURE

½ TSP CREAM OF TARTAR

½ TSP FINE SEA SALT

1 CUP/200 G SUPERFINE SUGAR

1 TSP PURE VANILLA EXTRACT

1¼ CUPS/175 G HAZELNUTS, TOASTED AND SKINNED (SEE PAGE 16), COARSELY CHOPPED

4 OZ/115 G BITTERSWEET CHOCOLATE, MELTED (SEE PAGE 17)

MAKES ABOUT 40 COOKIES

MERINGHE
ALLA
NOCCIOLA

Place the cooled meringues back on the parchment-lined baking sheets. Dip the tines of a fork into the melted chocolate and drizzle it back and forth over the cookies. Place the baking sheets in the freezer to let the chocolate set, about 5 minutes. The cookies will keep for up to 10 days in an airtight container stored at room temperature.

WHAT TO DRINK: Thick, bittersweet Italian-style hot chocolate.

NUTELLA
SANDWICH COOKIES

The dough for these cookies is rich and buttery, easy to assemble, and easy to roll out. What more could you want in a cookie—except for maybe a little Nutella, that delicious chocolate-hazelnut spread beloved by Italian children (and grown-ups)?

★

3 CUPS/380 G
UNBLEACHED
ALL-PURPOSE FLOUR

3 CUPS/300 G
CONFECTIONERS' SUGAR

¼ TSP FINE SEA SALT

FINELY GRATED ZEST OF
1 ORGANIC LEMON

FINELY GRATED ZEST OF
1 ORGANIC ORANGE

16 TBSP/225 G COLD
UNSALTED BUTTER, CUT
INTO ½-IN/12-MM CUBES

1 LARGE EGG, PLUS
2 EGG YOLKS

ABOUT 8 TBSP/150 G
NUTELLA

MAKES ABOUT
24
SANDWICH COOKIES

Put the flour, confectioners' sugar, salt, lemon zest, and orange zest in the work bowl of a food processor fitted with the metal blade. Pulse briefly to combine the ingredients. Distribute the butter pieces around the bowl and pulse until the mixture is crumbly. Add the egg and egg yolks and process until the dough just begins to come together.

Turn the dough out onto a lightly floured work surface and gather it together. Knead it briefly and shape it into a disk. Wrap tightly in plastic wrap and refrigerate for at least 1 hour, until well chilled.

Sprinkle a little flour onto the work surface and roll the disk out to ¼-in/6-mm thickness. Use your favorite cookie cutter shape to cut out cookies (I use a 2½-in/6-cm cutter with scalloped edges, which produces about 48 cookies). Place the cookies on ungreased baking sheets and chill for 30 minutes.

Heat the oven to 350°F/180°C. Bake the cookies in batches for 10 to 15 minutes, or until they are set and the edges are just beginning to brown. Transfer the baking sheets to cooling racks and let cool for 5 minutes. Using an offset spatula, remove the cookies from the baking sheets and let them cool completely on the racks.

Spread about 1 tsp of Nutella on the bottom of one cookie. Set another cookie on top of the filling and gently press the cookies together. Fill and sandwich together the remaining cookies. Arrange them on a decorative plate and serve. The cookies will keep up to 1 week in an airtight container stored at room temperature.

WHAT TO DRINK: Perfect for dunking in cold milk or, if you want to be adult about it, dipping in espresso.

OIL AND WINE
TARALLUCCI

FILLING

½ CUP/70 G
WHOLE ALMONDS,
TOASTED (SEE PAGE 16),
FINELY CHOPPED

1 CUP/340 G GOOD-
QUALITY, THICK GRAPE
JAM OR BLACKBERRY JAM

½ OZ/15 G BITTERSWEET
CHOCOLATE, GRATED

1½ TBSP UNSWEETENED
COCOA POWDER

½ TSP INSTANT ESPRESSO
POWDER

These old-fashioned jam-filled pockets are a specialty of Italy's Abruzzo region. This recipe was given to me by Fabrizio Lucci, who hosts tours of the beautiful area around the coastal city of Vasto. It's a specialty of his mother's, and I have her to thank for showing me how to mix and roll out the delicate dough and shape the cookies into fat rings. The traditional filling calls for scrucchjata, *a thick jam made in the fall from Montepulciano d'Abruzzo grapes. It's not easy to find outside of Italy, so I recommend either good artisanal grape jam (or your own homemade) or good blackberry jam, which has a similar winey quality. The dough, made with olive oil and wine, is very soft and not so easy to work with. But be persistent; you will get the hang of it, and it's well worth the effort because these are some of the flakiest, most delicate rustic cookies you'll ever bite into.*

Heat the oven to 350°F/180°C. Line two 11-by-17-in/28-by-43-cm rimmed baking sheets with parchment paper.

Make the filling: In a small bowl, combine the almonds, jam, grated chocolate, cocoa powder, and espresso powder. Fold everything together gently but thoroughly. Set aside.

Make the cookie dough: In a large bowl, stir together the olive oil and wine. Sprinkle in the flour a little at a time, stirring continuously with a fork to incorporate the ingredients. Continue to add flour and stir until you have a dough that is shiny, soft, and sticky, and just firm enough to handle. Turn the dough out onto a lightly floured work surface and knead until smooth and shiny, about 3 minutes.

Pinch off a small piece of dough—about the size of a walnut—and pat it into a small disk. Using a rolling pin, gently roll out the disk into an oval about 5 in/12 cm long and 3 in/8 cm wide. The dough will be sticky, but avoid adding too much additional flour, as it will toughen the dough. The best technique is to be confident and use a light touch so as not to tear the dough (if you tear the dough, press it back together; you don't want the filling to leak out).

Spread a thin layer of filling—less than 1 tsp—along the center of the piece of dough, leaving a border all around. Fold the long top edge over the filling to meet the bottom edge, and press gently but firmly to seal and to remove any air bubbles. Use a fluted pastry wheel to trim excess dough around the perimeter, leaving a thin border. Bring the two ends of the dough together to form a ring. Press the ends to seal. Set the cookie on a baking sheet. Continue to fill and shape the cookies and arrange them on the baking sheets, 15 per sheet. You should end up with 30 cookies. (Store any leftover filling in the refrigerator; it's great spread on toast or even as a filling for crêpes.)

Bake the cookies for 15 to 20 minutes, or until they are pale golden and just set. Transfer the baking sheets to cooling racks to cool for 5 minutes. Use an offset spatula to gently transfer the cookies to the racks to cool a bit more.

Arrange the cookies on a decorative platter and sprinkle generously with confectioners' sugar. Serve the cookies slightly warm or at room temperature. The cookies will keep for up to 1 week in an airtight container stored at room temperature.

WHAT TO DRINK: A dry red wine, such as Montepulciano d'Abruzzo.

COOKIE DOUGH

1 CUP/240 ML
EXTRA-VIRGIN OLIVE OIL

½ CUP/120 ML DRY
WHITE WINE

2½ TO 3 CUPS/300 TO
350 G "00" FLOUR
(SEE PAGE 15) OR
ALL-PURPOSE FLOUR

CONFECTIONERS' SUGAR
FOR DUSTING

MAKES ABOUT **30** COOKIES

PISTACHIO AMARETTI

★

1½ CUPS/180 G SHELLED
PISTACHIOS, SKINNED AND
TOASTED (SEE PAGE 16)

1 CUP/200 G
GRANULATED SUGAR

2 EGG WHITES

1 TSP PURE ALMOND
EXTRACT

CONFECTIONERS' SUGAR
FOR DUSTING

MAKES **20** COOKIES

These chewy cookies, with their pretty crackled tops, are traditionally made with almonds. Using pistachios instead gives them a nice toasty note and a subtle green hue, thanks to the extra step of skinning the nuts.

Line two 11-by-17-in/28-by-43-cm baking sheets with parchment paper.

Combine the pistachios and granulated sugar in the work bowl of a food processor fitted with the metal blade. Process for 2 to 3 minutes, or until the pistachios are very finely ground. With the motor running, pour in the egg whites and almond extract. Process until the mixture balls up around the blade. Continue to process until it relaxes a bit and becomes a very thick, sticky paste. It will be thick enough to scoop up with a spoon and hold its shape.

Using a spoon, drop mounds of batter (about 2 tsp per mound) 2 in/5 cm apart on the baking sheets. Smooth out the tops with lightly moistened fingers or a lightly moistened pastry brush. Let the cookies rest, uncovered, for 1 hour.

Heat the oven to 300°F/150°C. Bake the cookies, one sheet at a time, for about 20 minutes, or until they are set and slightly cracked on top and just beginning to brown around the edges. Transfer the baking sheets to cooling racks. Let the cookies cool completely before gently prying them off the parchment. Sift confectioners' sugar over the cookies before serving. The cookies will keep for up to 1 week in an airtight container stored at room temperature.

WHAT TO DRINK: Passito di Pantelleria, a sweet dessert wine.

RICCIARELLI

★

2½ CUPS/240 G
BLANCHED ALMOND FLOUR
OR MEAL (SEE PAGE 15)
OR VERY FINELY GROUND
BLANCHED ALMONDS

¾ CUP/150 G
GRANULATED SUGAR

1 CUP/100 G
CONFECTIONERS' SUGAR,
PLUS MORE FOR DUSTING

FINELY GRATED ZEST OF
1 ORGANIC ORANGE

2 EGG WHITES,
AT ROOM TEMPERATURE

1 TBSP HONEY

¼ TSP PURE ALMOND
EXTRACT

MAKES **34** TO **36** COOKIES

Pastry-shop windows all over Siena display piles of beautiful, sugar-coated almond cookies known as ricciarelli. These chewy diamond-shaped sweets date back to the Renaissance. Traditional ricciarelli are a bit of a chore to make, and the cookies, once shaped, must rest at room temperature overnight. These are my shortcut version, which take much less time but are, in my opinion, just as fit for Renaissance nobility.

Line three 11-by-17-in/28-by-43-cm rimmed baking sheets with parchment paper.

In a large bowl, whisk together the almond flour, the granulated sugar, ½ cup/50 g of the confectioners' sugar, and the orange zest. Take care to break up any clumps of almond flour.

In a small, clean stainless-steel bowl, beat the egg whites until they turn white and just start to billow. They should be soft, not stiff. Using a sturdy silicone spatula, scoop the egg whites into the large bowl and gently fold them into the almond mixture. Add the honey and almond extract and mix well, until you have a stiff, sticky paste.

Put the remaining ½ cup/50 g confectioners' sugar in a small shallow bowl. Pinch off a small piece of dough—about 2 tsp. Roll it into a ball and coat it thoroughly with the sugar. Using your fingers, gently press and pinch the ball into a rough diamond shape or an oval. Set it on a baking sheet. Continue to shape the cookies and set them on the baking sheets, 12 per sheet. Let the cookies sit, uncovered, for 1 to 2 hours to dry out a bit.

Heat the oven to 325°F/165°C. Bake the cookies for 12 minutes, or until their tops have cracked a bit and they are just barely tinged with pale gold around the edges. The cookies should hardly brown at all. Transfer the baking sheets to cooling racks and let the cookies cool completely.

Place the cookies on a decorative platter and dust with additional confectioners' sugar, if you like. The cookies will keep for up to 1 week in an airtight container stored at room temperature.

WHAT TO DRINK: Vin Santo, Tuscany's classic dessert wine.

ACKNOWLEDGMENTS

★ ★ ★

I didn't truly appreciate biscotti until I started baking them myself. They have become my essential after-dinner treat, my trusty morning-coffee companion, and the perfect afternoon pick-me-up. What fun I had working on this sweet book. I want to thank the folks who helped in its creation.

Bill LeBlond, for contributing that key first ingredient: the idea. I've enjoyed working with you.

Amy Treadwell and Dawn Yanagihara, for your valuable insights and for expertly guiding *Ciao Biscotti* through the editing process.

Abigail Bok, for your careful, eagle-eyed copyediting.

Peter Perez, David Hawk, Doug Ogan, and Tera Killip; as always, it is an honor and a pleasure to work with you.

Vanessa Dina, for mixing in the perfect amount of whimsy to your wonderful design.

Photographer Antonis Achilleos and food stylist Robin Lenzi for turning my recipes into such a visual treat.

Lisa Ekus and everyone at the Lisa Ekus Group, for your dedicated support of my work.

I'm fortunate to have the support of many wonderful friends and family. I am grateful to all of you. Special thanks to Maria Speck, champion of all things whole grain, for sharing her recipe for Walnut and Spelt biscotti; to Laura Kasavan, author of the beautiful blog Tutti Dolci, for sharing her recipe for Browned Butter and Toblerone biscotti; and Fabrizio Lucci for sharing his mother's treasured tarallucci recipe.

Thank you to my parents, Gabriella and Frank, who taught me to be proud of my heritage. And finally, to my husband, Scott, who contributed the drink pairings, and to Nick and Adriana, who despite not being nuts about nuts, proved to be the most diligent of taste testers—thanks to the three of you for sweetening my every day.

HAZELNUT OIL AND PISTACHIO OILS
La Tourangelle Artisan Oil
www.latourangelle.com
866-NUT-OILS (866-688-6457)

ITALIAN "OO" FLOUR
La Cuisine
www.lacuisineus.com
703-836-4435

BARLEY FLOUR AND SPELT FLOUR
Bob's Red Mill
www.bobsredmill.com
800-349-2173

DRIED TART CHERRIES AND TART CHERRY JUICE
Cherry Republic
www.cherryrepublic.com
800-206-6949

SWEET MATCHA POWDER
The Spice & Tea Exchange
www.spiceandtea.com
904-429-7548

INDEX